Supervising Student Teachers the Professional Way

SUPERVISING STUDENT TEACHERS THE PROFESSIONAL WAY

A Guide for Cooperating Teachers

THIRD EDITION

by

Marvin A. Henry, Ed.D.
Professor of Education
Chairperson, Department of Secondary Education
Indiana State University

and

W. Wayne Beasley, Ed.D.
Professor of Education
University of South Florida

Sycamore Press
P.O. Box 552
Terre Haute, Indiana 47808

III

Third Edition

Copyright © 1982 by Sycamore Press, P.O. Box 552, Terre Haute, IN 47808

ISBN 0-916768-05-8

Library of Congress Catalog Card No. 81-50782

To the Numerous Student Teachers Who Have Meandered Throughout These Pages:

May your journey have helped create a straighter path for those who are following you into the profession

MAH
WWB

PREFACE TO THE THIRD EDITION

The third edition of **Supervising Student Teachers the Professional Way** is designed to continue providing a practical reference for supervisors of student teachers and to update the content so that it remains germane to the task of directing student teachers. The authors define the terms in the title as follows:

Supervising means facilitating the growth of a future teacher through observation, analysis, conferences, and information sharing.

Student teachers are those teacher education candidates who are completing their final directed field experiences prior to completion of the sequence of professional study.

The professional way is considered to be a systematic process based on scientific knowledge and theoretical constructs.

This edition continues to emphasize the fact that the student teaching act involves development in the interpersonal, cognitive, and instructional processes. It reminds us that a student teacher must show growth in attitudes, values, and feelings as well as in the thinking processes, the selection of content and the determination of teaching strategies. A supervising teacher plays a key role in seeing that these domains are successfully developed throughout student teaching.

This edition has been extensively revised to reflect the changing conditions in the world of professional field experiences. Perhaps the most significant addition has been the inclusion of Chapter Ten, Legal Aspects of Supervising Student Teachers. The more complex legal world in education has had an impact on student teaching. The range of topics in this chapter should orient both the supervising teacher and student teacher to their roles, rights, and legal obligations.

More than one-fourth of all the case studies have been either revised or replaced in order to keep this popular feature current. In order to provoke further thinking, a series of questions has been added to each case study. The intent remains to confront the readers with typical situations involved in supervising student teachers and to encourage them to further investigate the problem at hand. The case situations presented are either real or composites of similar situations.

The worksheets which were interspersed in the chapters of the previous editions have been removed from chapter content, expanded, and placed in the Appendix along with some new forms. This format is designed to make these worksheets and forms more visible and usable.

Each chapter begins and closes with the imaginary Brian Sims and Elaine Bennett, student teacher and supervising teacher respectively. The introductory anecdote points to a problem relating to the chapter study and the closing narrative implies that the situation has been resolved. The chapter content is organized into sections with an attempt to provide practical information for the busy supervisor. Extensive use is made of italicized phrases which relate to a specific idea or concern. Busy supervisors may find them helpful for checking procedures or generating ideas. A summary set of principles is stated to reiterate the major ideas in the chapter. References are provided for those who wish to pursue a topic in greater detail.

The book is primarily designed as a textbook for university courses in principles and techniques of supervising student teachers with the intent that it will accompany teachers into their classrooms where they supervise student teachers. However, classroom teachers can effectively use it as a reference in the event that they are asked to supervise student teachers without the benefit of a formal course in supervision. Public school administrators and college supervisors will find that it is valuable as a reference for overseeing student teaching programs.

When we initiated the project of writing the first edition of this book more than a dozen years ago, we were convinced that a practical reference book for supervising teachers would be beneficial in the educational field. We still believe this to be true and assume that this edition keeps pace with new developments in student teacher supervision.

Marvin A. Henry
W. Wayne Beasley

Acknowledgments

The authors are indebted to many people who have assisted in the preparation of this edition. The comments of numerous colleagues across the nation have been solicited and their suggestions have been implemented throughout the book. The authors appreciate the reactions from teachers and professors who have used the previous editions and have taken time to offer suggestions for improvement. The contribution of Lauretta Holderread, doctoral fellow at Indiana State University, who did extensive library analysis in updating of the references must be recognized. The editorial work of Ruth Henry has helped to eliminate obfuscation and to make the book much more readable. Finally, the work of Vera Yeager, who typed, and typed, and typed without complaint is greatly appreciated.

MAH
WWB

CONTENTS

Chapter One

BEFORE THE STUDENT TEACHING EXPERIENCE BEGINS

Elaine Bennett carefully studied a note from her principal which requested that she supervise a student teacher from State University during the next semester. When she talked with him about accepting such a responsibility, he assured her that he felt she was capable of performing the role.

Feeling somewhat inadequate for such a task, she hoped that she could quickly learn something about what it means to supervise a student teacher. The principal suggested that she talk to some of the other teachers in the building who had previously supervised student teachers in order to learn more about the process. She learned from the university correspondence that the student would make a pre-teaching visit to the school prior to the beginning of the experience and she wondered what she should do to prepare for this meeting.

A few days later, Brian Sims, a teacher education major at State University, received a form which revealed his student-teaching assignment. He stared at its contents and with a puzzled look inquired to all within hearing distance, "Do any of you know anything about Central City?" Later on, he received a briefing on student teaching responsibilities in a meeting with a university supervisor. The orientation concluded with the requirement for a school visit in order to become familiar with the teaching situation and to meet the supervising teacher.

Brian wrote a brief request to Miss Bennett to visit on a specific day. He raised several questions in the letter about his teaching and indicated that he desired to learn more about his responsibilities, the community, the school, and the pupils. Miss Bennett carefully folded the correspondence and began to consider what she could do to help this stranger become acquainted with the school and with her class . .

STUDENT TEACHER SUPERVISION: Presiding over a Professional Transition

In a few short weeks of student teaching a college student completes the final developmental phase in becoming a teacher and refines the skills and attitudes that will inaugurate a teaching career. This transformation occurs not on the college campus under the watchful eye of a professor but takes place in an elementary or secondary school under the direction of a classroom teacher.

A teacher who agrees to supervise a student teacher has consented to assume one of the most responsible, influential and exciting positions in teacher education. This brief period in the life of a college student has greater impact on professional skills and potential than any other part of a college career.

There is evidence which shows that the teaching model established by the supervising teacher becomes the actual pattern followed by the student teacher.[1] It is a stimulating experience for a teacher to have a student teacher in the classroom because pupils seem to learn more when a student teacher is available to work with a class. In spite of the increased responsibility involved, the experience of student teaching is a winning proposition for all parties.

The period of student teaching may be the only time that an undergraduate has the benefit of individualized instruction. This offers a unique opportunity for the supervising teacher to demonstrate one-to-one instruction which is one of the most highly regarded of all teaching techniques. The hours together provide time for analysis, feedback, information-sharing, planning, and evaluation. These activities are the nucleus for effective learning and they can be adapted to the student's individual needs.

A classroom is modified when a student teacher arrives. A teacher who has been solely in charge of a class will be working jointly and sharing responsibility with a person who is a capable but less experienced instructor. A student teacher will assume much of the responsibility which has previously been the prerogative of a teacher. Eventually a teacher surrenders a great amount of teaching activity and autonomy to this neophyte and assumes the role of supervisor and counselor.

Experience - The Key to Success

The objective of a professional certification program is to prepare a teaching candidate to be competent in specialized knowledge and professional skills. The final development of such skills ultimately involves experience in a classroom setting which is supervised by a classroom teacher. The culminating activity in this sequence is student teaching.

Experience at this level is a very sophisticated process and should not be confused with all activity which transpires in a class. When a teaching candidate is learning to teach through experience, the classical processes of the scientific method are brought into play. A problem arises and reflection begins. A student teacher learns to analyze the problem and to devise and consider alternatives which should improve the situation. A solution is then implemented and its results are observed.

[1]Samuel Brodbelt, "Selecting the Supervising Teacher," **Contemporary Education** 51:2, 86-88, Winter, 1980.

The function of a student teaching program is to structure an environment in which a teaching candidate can actually attempt to direct learning, to reflect upon that experience, and to develop patterns of behavior which will be more successful in guiding learning experiences.

Through the process of guided activity a student teacher develops the ability to function in the world of the first-year teacher. It is a challenging responsibility and an exciting process and may be the main reason why teachers are willing to work with student teachers.

A Challenging Professional Atmosphere

A classroom containing a student teacher creates a challenging professional atmosphere. A student teacher can be an asset in many different instructional situations throughout all the weeks of the experience. Trenfield[2] cites eight specific ways in which a student teacher's presence may improve classroom instruction:

1. The presence of a student teacher in the classroom frequently is stimulating to both pupils and teacher.
2. The presence of a student teacher requires the supervising teacher to examine critically his own objectives and teaching strategies.
3. The student teacher is sometimes a valuable source of ideas about instructional techniques and materials.
4. Until the student teacher assumes responsibility for most of the instruction, there are two teachers in the classroom, enabling them to work as a team to plan and conduct activities.
5. While the student teacher conducts class, the supervising teacher is able to observe his student from a different perspective, perhaps gaining valuable insight into his interests and learning problems.
6. While the student teacher conducts classes the supervising teacher may work with individuals and small groups who need more special attention than he can normally find time to give them.
7. As the student teacher assumes more responsibility the supervising teacher is freed to consult administrators and colleagues, to accumulate instructional materials, and to plan instruction for the future.

[2]William Trenfield, "Your Student Teacher: An Asset in the Classroom?" **Supervisors Quarterly** 6:2, Winter, 1970-71, p. 34.

8. Occasionally a pupil will relate much better to one adult than to another. The presence of a student teacher gives this pupil additional opportunity to form a meaningful relationship with an adult.

The presence of a student teacher presents an excellent inservice activity for the supervising teacher. If student teaching is approached by both student teacher and supervising teacher as an opportunity for growth, the possibilities for improved instruction are countless. The supervising teacher should start to think of the possibilities before the student teacher arrives.

PREPARING FOR A STUDENT TEACHER: Building a Good Beginning

It is just as essential to prepare for the arrival of a student teacher as it is to prepare to teach a new class. Adequate preparation reduces anxiety and provides a smooth introduction of the student teacher into teaching.

A great number of arrangements will be necessary before a student teacher arrives on the scene. Effective preparation includes knowledge of the requirements of a student teaching program, making adjustments to allow for participation by a student teacher, and developing the concept of working on a team basis with a teaching candidate.

The supervising teacher will have to be prepared to make modifications in order to assimilate a new personality into the classroom routine. The individuality of a student teacher is a variable that can determine the types of responsibilities which will be assumed. The confident, outgoing student may be able to readily adjust to most situations, but the timid or insecure person may need responsibilities which build confidence. An alert supervising teacher will want to know something about the incoming student teacher in order to plan for the most appropriate initial activities.

Learning About a Student Teacher

It is advantageous to become acquainted with a future student teacher as soon as possible through personal contact and written communication. This knowledge will increase understanding and decrease the possibility of making incorrect judgments. The following information will be helpful:

Educational background
   High school record
   College courses completed in major and minor areas
   General education
   Experiences with children or young people
   Prior field experiences
General experiences
   Employment
   Community service
   Leadership responsibilities
   Travel
Personal characteristics
   Age
   Health status
   Recreational interests
   Marital status
Family background
Autobiographical statement
Participation in campus activities
Professional goals

A considerable amount of information is normally summarized by the student when application is made for student teaching, and the university student teaching office typically forwards this resume to the school. If it has not been made available, an inquiry to the individual who is charged with the assignment of student teachers in the school will probably reveal whether it has been forwarded by the university.

All information received in written form may be supplemented and interpreted through informal conferences with the student teacher and with those who know him at the university. Information should be secured only for the purpose of helping to know more about a student teacher in order to better understand the professional needs and potential of this person.

Preparing the Class

A teacher should begin to establish a student teacher's status with the class before the arrival date. The pupils ought to know that a student teacher is coming and should anticipate this event with some eagerness. Typical preparation will include:

Creating anticipation that more interesting, worthwhile experiences will be possible

Cite knowledge or skills which a student teacher may possess.

Refer to activities that might be achieved while two teachers are available.

Make plans for some ambitious and exciting projects.

Initiating correspondence between the class and the student teacher

Class members could introduce themselves through a letter.

Class members could write encouraging comments such as "I wish you success," etc.

Class members could indicate goals which they hope they can achieve while the student teacher is with them.

Class members might make some requests which would utilize university resources which the student teacher might have available.

The student teacher might be encouraged to write a letter of introduction describing preparation, interests, and experiences which would be related to the work of the class.

Describing the purposes of student teaching

Differences between regular teaching and student teaching

Goals and skills which the student teacher should achieve

Explaining how the members of the class can help the student teacher

Cooperation

Interest

Case Study No. 1: WE DO NOT WANT A STUDENT TEACHER

When you informed your class that a student teacher was coming, you received a chorus of grumbles. Instead of showing enthusiasm, the students expressed complaints which seemed to communicate feelings of not wanting any changes in the class.

The student teaching candidate will be here for an initial visit within a few days. What will you do to try to change this class attitude?

1. Instruct them to either cooperate or suffer consequences.

2. Pretend that you feel that they do not mean what they say.
3. Re-examine your decision about accepting a student teacher.
4. Begin a systematic approach which will show how a student teacher will make the classroom better.
5. _____

Comment:

     This reaction may be a compliment to your teaching or an expression of insecurity. If it is the latter, some attention may need to be given to preparing the students to deal with change. Examine the way in which the statement was made and see if there is an alternative procedure which will cause pupils to anticipate this new student's arrival rather than to dread it.

Questions:

1. What would you do if they cheer the announcement that a student teacher will be coming to take over some of your responsibilities?
2. What causes pupils to resist a change of teachers?

Preparing the Student Teacher

It can be assumed that student teachers will have received some orientation to student teaching at the university, but there are certain types of preparation that can only be accomplished at the cooperating school by the supervising teacher. For example, the future student teacher may have questions about the activities and responsibilities of this new assignment. The following are typical:

Where is the school located?
Where does a visitor report upon arrival at school?
What are the nature and composition of the classes?
What information about the community should be known initially?
What kind of advance preparation would be helpful?

A student teacher can benefit from having answers to the above questions before the initial visit is made. A letter which contains a set of directions to the school and stating where visitors report can be useful and reassuring.

There may be several creative ways to describe the class. A statement of class sizes and content being studied is a good beginning. Consider also having students write a brief note of introduction or welcome. Better yet include photographs or perhaps cassette recordings which the student teacher can listen to. Such gestures can help to create a sense of belonging.

Finally, offer a few substantive thoughts which may cause a student teacher to perceive what contributions can be made. Encourage thought about teaching ideas or resources. Suggest that a real difference will be made if work is begun early on certain topics which are to be taught.

THE PRE-TEACHING VISIT: **Strangers Become Colleagues**

A pre-teaching visit is a routine part of student teaching procedure and it may occur several days or several weeks in advance of the date of the actual experience. Directions for this contact from the university may be highly structured or extremely informal. In either case it is important to remember that mutual impressions are being formed and that these reactions are very fundamental to future working relationships.

The pre-teaching visit should be a work session rather than a social call. The student teacher will want to visit classes, become acquainted with the supervisor, and meet key school personnel. This time will provide the opportunity to clarify some points of concern which are not clear to either party. The major tasks of this visit are summarized as follows:

Determine a teaching load for student teaching
Become acquainted with instructional materials
Learn something about the students
Discuss and plan initial teaching activities

It is important for this new participant to become involved at this initial stage. Since a student teacher will likely have many questions and concerns, there should be ample opportunity for dialogue. A student will undoubtedly be more comfortable if allowed to make a contribution. The pre-teaching visit must be more than classroom observation.

In the event that a pre-teaching visit is not made, the above activity must be accomplished very quickly at the beginning of the student-teaching experience. It will also be beneficial to redouble efforts in prior communication by providing as much information as possible so that the student teacher knows as much about the school and the pupils as possible.

Case Study No. 2: THE VISITOR IS RELUCTANT TO BECOME INVOLVED IN ACTIVITY

You were expecting that a student teacher would indicate that there would be much to learn through student teaching, but you were not prepared for what happened during the pre-teaching visit. She appeared extremely insecure and confessed that she was not familiar with the subject matter you were teaching since it had been a while since she had taken any course in that area. She was reluctant to participate in any class activities and seemed not to want to become involved. You further observed that she avoided the pupils as much as possible in the informal moments.

What action should you take?

1. Do nothing at the present since this is the first contact.
2. Investigate her record for clues to this kind of behavior.
3. Attempt to structure some activity so that she will receive positive reinforcement.
4. Give her some materials to study before she returns for student teaching.
5. Introduce her to pupils so that she can get to know them as individuals.
6. Notify the university of your concerns.
7. _____

Comment:

The student teacher's expressions seem to indicate a feeling of inadequacy. The teacher might begin by assessing the dynamics of the classroom situation to see if there are factors which encourage the student teacher to feel timid. The supervising teacher could also consider designing activities which would help the student to feel secure in the classroom.

Questions:

1. What is the greatest problem in this situation?
2. Can an insecure-appearing person succeed in teaching?

PROVIDING INFORMATION ABOUT THE SCHOOL AND COMMUNITY: **The Welcome Wagon Comes to School**

The school environment may be more strange to the student teacher than one would suppose. A supervising teacher who has lived in the community and taught in its school system for some time may assume that the student teacher is also familiar with the environment. There is a sizable amount of information that will aid the newcomer in understanding the school community, and it will be helpful if the supervisor has prepared to share this knowledge with the student teacher. Depending on the individual situation, attention should be called to the following:

Information about the school in general
  Type of population served
  Philosophy and objectives
  Unique characteristics, facilities, or services
School policies relating to the teachers and student teachers
  Arrival time
  Reporting absences
School policies relating to the students
  Dress
  Discipline
  Student activities
Forms and reports which must be completed
  Grade forms
  Attendance reports
Emergency procedures
  Fires
  Weather
Specific information about pupils
  Pupil records
  Personality characteristics
School schedule of classes
  Schedule deviations
School directory
School calendar

Location of the classroom in relation to the office, work rooms, cafeteria, teachers' lounge, rest rooms, and library
Service facilities
    Procedure for reproducing materials
    Audio-visual services and resources
    Supplies
Teacher responsibilities in the extracurricular program
    Types of duties
    Compensation

    There are several methods of acquainting a student teacher with the responsibilities of teaching before becoming a full-time participant. A school handbook, for instance, is quite beneficial in helping a student teacher understand the school. In the absence of or in addition to this information some administrators provide orientation programs for prospective student teachers which help acquaint them with the many important facets of the school. Other faculty members may be willing to help with initial orientation. The pre-teaching visit provides a good opportunity for introductions to teachers who will voluntarily assist the student teacher in getting acquainted with the school.

    A community handbook which is often available from a local service organization can be useful. If such a publication is unavailable, the supervisor may want to describe those facilities which will be necessary or useful to the student teacher. The following list is typical of the student teacher's needs in learning more about a new area:

Living accommodations
Restaurants
Available transportation
Recreational facilities
Places of interest
Service facilities
Location of shopping areas
Unique features
Community social structure

    A checklist for student teacher preparation is found in the Appendix as Worksheet Number One. Teachers may find it to be beneficial in completing the details which are necessary before the student teacher arrives.

Case Study No. 3: STRANGER IN THE PROMISED LAND

During Alan's pre-teaching visit he expressed concern about the community. He asked several leading questions about the run-down appearance of the section of the city where your school is located and wondered what the students would be like. He contrasted the school with his home school which he described in complimentary terms. He implied that his background was quite different from your students and wondered if he could communicate with them.

How do you respond?

1. Defend the community and the school.
2. Ignore the comments and try to direct his attention to the teaching concerns that will occupy his time.
3. Try to get him acquainted with students, hoping that he will have a more favorable attitude.
4. Suggest that a new situation normally causes some anxiety and that he will soon become accustomed to the school and community.
5. _____

Comment:

Alan's surface feelings may result from fears or agitation. If he is a bit anxious about his ability, he may be looking for reasons which would justify his performance in a strange setting. If he did not wish to be assigned to the school, he may be projecting unhappiness with university personnel who are responsible for the placement. His attitude will probably change most quickly through understanding and through involvement which will give him a feeling of achievement. A warm greeting from teachers and students can be very reassuring, and a newcomers packet could alter his opinion of the community.

Questions:

1. What are some methods of introducing a student teacher to a different type of school community?
2. Is it likely that the actual differences are as great as the student teacher indicates?

Brian Sims guided his automobile into the faculty parking lot and eased into a space reserved for visitors. After hastily checking a few papers, he walked quickly to the main entrance of the school and followed the signs to the principal's office.

A few minutes later, Miss Bennett is greeted at her door by the principal who introduces the new student teacher from State University.

"Hello, Brian," said Miss Bennett with a smile, "welcome to Central City."

As the principal returned to the office, Miss Bennett and Brian moved into the classroom.

"I'm glad you are here," began Miss Bennett, "I hope we can make some plans for your teaching, and I would like to know something of your particular interests. I also want to give you a tour of the building so that you will know about our facilities before you begin student teaching."

"I appreciate this opportunity," replied the visitor. "I still have several questions about my responsibilities, and I would like to know about your students so that I can make some plans while I have university resources available."

The conversation continued until late in the afternoon. Brian was seen leaving the building carrying a stack of books and papers. His small car moved smoothly out of the parking lot, apparently headed for a quick tour of the downtown area before returning to the campus.

Remember:

More anxiety may occur prior to student teaching than during the actual experience.

Little information about the school or the supervising teacher may be provided to the student teacher before the first contact with the school.

The supervising teacher determines the classroom atmosphere and activity structure before the student teacher arrives.

The best orientation plans will result in having a student teacher involved as a participating faculty member.

Student teaching is a period of transition in which the teaching candidate changes from college student to beginning teacher.

Student teaching is a process not an end product.

USEFUL REFERENCES

BENNIE, WILLIAM A., **Supervising Clinical Experiences in the Classroom,** Harper and Row, 1972, pp. 10-15, 52-63, 66-72.

BLASER, FRANK and McEWIN, TOM, "Student Teachers Strengthen Your Schools," **ISBA Journal** 16:5, pp. 3-4, May, 1970.

BRODBELT, SAMUEL, "Selecting the Supervising Teacher," **Contemporary Education** 51:2, pp. 86-88, Winter, 1980.

CARUSO, JOSEPH J., "Phases in Student Teaching," **Young Children** 33: 57-63, November, 1977.

CHURCH, KENNETH R., "The Making of a Teacher: Guidelines for the Teacher Education Institution and the Cooperating Teacher," **The Physical Educator** 33: 26-9, March, 1976.

CLOTHIER, GRANT, and KINGSLEY, ELIZABETH, **Enriching Student Teaching Relationships,** Midwest Educational Training and Research Organization, pp. 5, 10-12.

DIVINE, JUDY, "Guidelines for Supervisors of Student Teachers," **School and Community** 60, p. 12, November, 1973.

ELKIND, BARBARA, "Going to Be a Cooperating Teacher? Be the Best!" **Instructor** 86: 81-3, October, 1976.

HENRY, MARVIN A., "Supervising Teachers Report Attitudes Concerning Selected Aspects of Student Teaching," **Supervisors Quarterly** 6:3, pp. 33-36, Spring, 1971.

HORTON, LOWELL, "What to Do Before the Student Teacher Arrives," **Illinois Education,** pp. 72-73, December, 1970.

MAHAN, JAMES M., "Endorsement and Practice of Selected Principles for the Supervision of Student Teaching," **The Teacher Educator** 7:3, pp. 28-36, Spring, 1972.

MYERS, PAUL E., "Anatomy of a Supervisor," **The Teacher Educator** 13: 35-7, Winter, 1977-78.

ODDO, MICHELE, and COX, BARBARA, **Take Me Under Your Wing,** Professional Improvement Series for Supervising Teachers, College of Education, Northern Illinois University, DeKalb, IL., 1979 (slide/tape).

SCHUMANN, HERBERT, "Better University Supervisors and Cooperating Teachers," **Agricultural Education** 49: 81, 83, October, 1976.

SEYMOUR, JIM; KEARL, STAN, and WILSON, DAVID, **Meet Your Supervising Teacher,** Professional Improvement Series for Supervising Teachers, College of Education, Northern Illinois University, DeKalb, IL., 1979 (slide/tape).

SPANJER, R. ALLAN, **Teacher Preparation: Supervision and Performance,** Association of Teacher Educators, 1972, pp. 4-7.

TRENFIELD, WILLIAM, "Your Student Teacher: An Asset in the Classroom?" **Supervisors Quarterly** 6:2, 35-39, Winter, 1970-71.

Chapter Two

THE STUDENT TEACHER'S FIRST FEW DAYS

Brian Sims arrived early at the school on his first day of student teaching. Making his way down the hall, he arrived at Miss Bennett's room just as she entered carrying a stack of papers. After the initial greetings, they engaged in small talk while they waited for the school day to begin.

Brian attempted to appear at ease, but he failed to conceal his tensions. All the information given him the previous week in orientation at the university seemed to whirl around in his head as the school emitted the sounds of a busy Monday morning. Appearance! Requirements! Ethics! Teaching! Observations! Planning! Organization! Student behavior! The orientation instructions seemed more remote and abstract as the actual situation was encountered, and he clenched the arm of his chair as the minute hand pointed to the top of the hour.

The complexity of the supervisory task became more apparent to Miss Bennett as she talked with her beginning student teacher. So much was at stake for him. She was a little uneasy herself since this was a new experience for her also. Many details had to be attended to quickly, but the first task which had to be performed was to acquaint the class with its student teacher. The bell sounded and attendance was checked quickly. She arose from her desk more carefully than usual, looked at her pupils, and began to introduce her first student teacher to the class. . .

THE FIRST FEW DAYS: Adjustment, Learning, and Demands

Pre-teaching visits and communication cause some preparedness for the impending change caused by the presence of a student teacher, but only physical presence provides the full impact of this different educational climate. The arrival of a student teacher brings about a change in the classroom environment which is sensed by both pupils and teacher.

The first few days are periods of adjustment and learning for the student teacher who is confronted with a whole new series of tasks which may cause apprehensive and awkward feelings. If the early experiences of a student teacher are successful, subsequent responsibilities will pose much less threat. During these initial days the student teacher has a number of tasks to meet:

To become acquainted with school personnel
To get to know the students
To become aware of the curriculum
To become familiar with the classroom routine
To assume some teaching responsibility

Early experiences tend to set the mode of procedure for student teaching. In an investigation of teaching styles of student teachers and their cooperating teachers, Seperson and Joyce[1] found that the relationship established during the initial part of student teaching continued throughout the entire semester. The tasks listed above appear more significant when one contemplates the impact that they have for the entire experience.

The pupils will also begin a period of adjustment to the new classroom personality. What is this new person like? What changes will there be? They will observe the supervising teacher's reaction to the student teacher. Some pupils will vie for the attention of this new individual and the supervising teacher may note that a few persons are acting differently. A new mood may permeate the entire classroom.

The supervising teacher should be ready to accept additional responsibilities. The most apparent initial change may be the different work load that must be assumed. During the first few days, he will need to:

Confer with the student teacher and provide orientation to the school
Plan constructive activities which will involve the student teacher
Introduce the student teacher to various members of the faculty and staff
Confer with the college supervisor when he visits
Acquaint the student teacher with procedures involved in planning and preparation
Begin to determine a teaching schedule for the student teacher
Arrange initial teaching activities and observations
Become familiar with the university's requirements for the student teaching program

INTRODUCING THE STUDENT TEACHER TO THE CLASS: Helping Strangers Meet New Friends

An introduction of a student teacher does more than present a name to a group of pupils or give the student teacher a chance to offer greetings to a sea of faces. It is a process of communicating feelings and ascribing status. This may be the

---

[1]Marvin A. Seperson, and Bruce R. Joyce, "Teaching Styles of Student Teachers as Related to Those of Their Cooperating Teachers," **Educational Leadership Research Supplement** 31:146-51, November, 1973.

most obvious clue for the pupils in perceiving their teacher's attitude toward this beginner. Certain words in the introduction can reveal what the supervising teacher actually thinks of the student teacher.

The introduction often is the activity which defines the roles of student teacher, supervising teacher, and pupils. Since it may affect relationships during the entire student teaching sequence, it should be carefully planned. These considerations are worthy of emphasis in designing an effective introduction:

Welcome the student teacher
> Project the feelings of sincerity and delight at having this person as part of the class
> Use personal expressions to show a feeling of acceptance
> Ask pupils to share in the greeting

Recognize the competency of a student teacher
> Specify major areas of study
> Describe any particular experiences or achievements related to areas of study
> Mention interesting skills the student teacher possesses

Introduce the student as a teacher
> Show that he has status and authority

Indicate confidence in the student teacher
> Project the feeling that he can work successfully in the classroom

Make the introduction open-ended
> Give the student teacher an opportunity to speak to the class

The student teacher should be introduced to the class in a way which gives status and conveys a feeling of welcome. It may be a formal introduction or a more personal presentation, but it should contain appropriate elements of the above criteria. In either event, the student teacher should not simply enter the classroom and begin. A good introduction will help to establish the person as a teacher in the class.

Case Study No. 4: THE STUDENT TEACHER USES HIS INTRODUCTION TO EXPLAIN HIS RULES

Steve had displayed some signs of being apprehensive but you were not concerned because you had anticipated some initial reservations. He had indicated fear of being able to control a class and you had suggested that he should be firm in the beginning. You did not realize how literally he would consider this advice until he made his response to your introduction. Without consulting you he used this initial appearance to spell out several rules and regulations which he would expect the students to obey. Some of these directions conflict with your procedures and others simply could not be enforced.

What would you do?
1. Make no effort to do anything and assume that things will work out.
2. Talk with him after class and suggest a revised set of comments for the next contact with the students.
3. Attempt to change the introductory statements by interjecting some interpretive remarks as you follow up on his comments.
4. Correct him during the introduction.
5. Affirm to the class that the student teacher is in charge when he is teaching and that he will have complete authority in the classroom.
6. _____

Comment:
    Student teachers and beginning teachers are frequently admonished to be tough in the beginning and then relax their standards after control has been established. This is his effort to convince the pupils that he intends to be in control and demand respect, but it may actually be a result of his feeling of insecurity. The supervising teacher must be alert to see that the student teacher becomes secure without alienating the class. This incident presents such a challenge.

Questions:
1. Is it a good idea to advise student teachers to be tough initially?
2. Has any real damage been done in regard to classroom management?
3. What is the student teacher likely to do next?

Case Study No. 5: THE STUDENT TEACHER PRO-
JECTS UNCERTAINTY IN GREETING THE CLASS

Kim was quite timid. She had answered questions quickly and hesitated to look directly at you when talking. She appeared reluctant to respond to an introduction on the first day, but you felt that it was necessary that she greet the class. After you introduce her, she mumbles a few words and sits down quickly. The students appear a bit surprised and look at each other dubiously. Then they look at you. What do you do?

1. Continue as if the response was what you had expected.
2. Attempt to involve the student teacher in conversation with you and the class.
3. Mention a specific topic that she is familiar with and ask her to talk about it.
4. Fabricate a reason for her making a hasty response.
5. Arrange to be alone with the class soon and explain that she is a learner and determine how you and the class can work together to help her.
6. _____

Comment:

Probably everyone in the room including Kim will be wondering about the supervising teacher's reaction. The teacher's next moves may well determine the pattern of future reactions. In most situations the student teacher would be best supported by a teacher's acting as if the response were natural. However, this does not relieve the supervising teacher of the responsibility of working to help this insecure person to relax in subsequent situations of this kind.

Questions:

1. What can be done to anticipate and avoid this problem?
2. Would a perceptive teacher have known that this situation was likely to occur?

Case Study No. 6: THE EAGER BEAVER

Your student teacher possessed confidence in herself. After your introduction she makes an enthusiastic response:

"Boys and girls, I'm so glad to be here. I've been looking forward to working with you, and I have a lot of new ideas and games for you. I just know we're going to have a great time together! We are going to do some things that have not been done before. You are going to love them because I am going to see that you do."

What is your response?
1. Make no comment about the introduction.
2. Endorse the student teacher's enthusiasm.
3. Attempt to tone down her comments in your subsequent remarks to the class.
4. Give the class an opportunity to interact with her.
5. _____

Comment:
Educational literature indicates that most student teachers are anxious to begin teaching. Obviously, here is a person who is enthusiastic but naive. She may have made some erroneous assumptions about the latitude to do what she wants.

Questions:
1. How do supervising teachers innocently encourage such feelings?
2. How would your class respond to such an introduction?
3. What are the desirable features of an introduction like this?

INTRODUCING THE STUDENT TEACHER TO THE FACULTY: Meeting the Charter Members

The process of becoming a teacher involves relationships with other professionals. A student teacher's previous contacts with teachers have been as a student; now they are associates. It may be surprising to learn that most of them are friendly and sincere and even possess human frailties. There is much that can be learned about teaching through association with colleagues.

The encouragement and assistance of teachers on a school staff can mean much to a beginner. They can provide instructional ideas for the student teacher and make substantial impressions which will affect his outlook toward the teaching profession. Some faculty members may have a special interest in the student teacher. This is particularly likely among those who were graduated from the same college and those who teach the same grade levels or subject areas. A student teacher may be sought out because he can often contribute knowledge and ideas to the instructional staff.

The introduction to the faculty should be made in a manner that will provide recognition and acceptance of the student teacher. The following procedures may be of value in considering a desirable method of acquainting the student teacher with members of the faculty:

Make it known that a student teacher is coming to work with you
> The official school announcement or school newspaper can list the names and arrival dates of student teachers.
> The impending arrival of a student teacher can be mentioned in casual conversation with teachers.

Introduce the student teacher to the faculty
> Faculty meetings
> Informal get-togethers where student teachers can meet the staff

Make comments that will help a student teacher know and remember a teacher
> Indicate a faculty member's responsibilities and make comments that will serve as cues in recalling that person.

Arrange a time to be spent with other teachers without your presence

.

Case Study No. 7: COMMENTS FROM THE TEACHERS' LOUNGE SURPRISE THE STUDENT TEACHER

You had suggested that the student teacher spend some time in the teachers' lounge to become acquainted with teachers. After a few visits, he became negative about teachers because they constantly criticize students and make caustic comments about school administrators. He cannot understand their cynicism about teaching in general. He was really shocked when one teacher told him that if he were wise he would not go into teaching.

How do you respond?
1. Suggest that he stay away from the lounge.
2. Explain that these are the minutes when teachers relax and that their comments should not always be taken literally.
3. Explain that not all teachers follow a strict code of ethics.
4. Talk to the teachers involved when you have the opportunity and inform them of their effect upon the student teacher's attitudes.
5. _____

Comment:
A student teacher may not be prepared to accept the fact that teachers possess many of the same weaknesses as other mortals. Many student teachers will be more idealistic and optimistic than the classroom veterans. The chief task may be that of reconciling their idealism with the fact that teachers' comments in their informal moments do not necessarily indicate what they actually practice in the classroom.

Questions:
1. How can a student teacher come to accept teachers informally?
2. How much guidance should be provided in teacher contact?
3. Should a supervising teacher attempt to have a student teacher avoid the negative and ineffective teachers in the building?

INTRODUCING THE STUDENT TEACHER TO TEACHING: **Gingerly into the Stream**

The student teacher's initiation into the classroom is critical. The first few days can easily become boring and anxious for the student teacher and these feelings may remain until he is convinced that he has been accepted and is actually working as a teacher.

Boredom results from inactivity. Most student teachers have been active in college and are prepared for the same kind of intense schedule at their assigned school. A well intentioned supervising teacher can contribute to boredom by falsely assuming that a student teacher should observe a while before assuming any kind of classroom responsibility. A student teacher may lose interest in a matter of hours if there is nothing to do that seems to be of significance. The best antidote for boredom and anxiety is meaningful activity.

The Initial Days

The first day of student teaching is not too early for the student teacher to be involved in classroom participation, but responsibilities should be given which will make a contribution to the class. There are many worthwhile teaching activities which can be performed without intensive preparation or orientation. Possible early activities include:

Carrying out brief teaching activities
Distributing and collecting papers
Checking attendance
Supervising study periods
Supervising a recess period
Administering tests and quizzes
Assisting with laboratory or project work
Working with individuals or small groups
Operating equipment
Assisting the teacher with demonstrations
Explaining a specific procedure or technique
Planning and creating a display or bulletin board

A student teacher will find it advantageous to be seated in front of the room beginning the first day at school. This location helps to establish that a teacher rather than a visitor is in the room. It increases awareness of classroom dynamics and will facilitate the task of learning the names of the pupils in the class. A teacher is more likely to seek the assistance of a nearby student teacher in minor but necessary teaching tasks such as writing on the chalkboard or distributing papers. In effect the student teacher becomes a second teacher in the room.

The student teacher will be formulating impressions about the nature of the class during these first few days. He will observe the supervisor's procedures and probably start to develop his own style. The student teacher will respond favorably to the supervisor's taking time to explain his actions or to analyze the results of a particular situation.

A suitable teaching schedule should be determined early. It will first be helpful for the student teacher to know what has been taught previously, what is to be taught during the weeks of student teaching, and what will be covered after the experience. This information should be combined with available resources so that familiarity with content and thought concerning teaching will evolve. Obviously some early conferences on this topic are required.

There are many activities which must be completed by the supervising teacher in the initial days. Some teachers feel a need to know what should be done and what has been done. Worksheet Number Two in the Appendix provides a checklist which can be used either for preparing for the initial days or for reviewing the adequacy of the orientation program. Teachers who wish such assistance will find the checklist to be helpful.

Case Study No. 8: TOO ANXIOUS TO BEGIN TEACHING

Cindy is enthusiastic. She says that she is excited about student teaching and wants to begin immediately. She asks if she can teach her entire teaching schedule on the second day so that she will know what it is like. You have serious reservations, but she is persistent and you do not want to crush her enthusiasm. You are in a real dilemma concerning this request.

What action do you take?
1. Let her teach as much as she wishes and then wait to see if any problems result.
2. Counter with the proposal that she begin with smaller amounts of activity and then assume additional tasks as she becomes more capable.
3. Indicate that your policy is for a student teacher to observe a number of days before assuming responsibility for a class.
4. _____

Comment:
One of the mistakes supervising teachers commonly make is to wait too long before permitting a student teacher to become involved in teaching. But a problem which can be nearly as disastrous

is to give too much teaching responsibility too soon. It is unlikely that a student teacher's enthusiasm will be dealt a permanent blow if she teaches less than she wants during the first few days. It is possible that a capable student teacher can assume a heavier schedule immediately, but this is not likely.

Questions:
1. How can one distinguish between enthusiasm alone and enthusiasm based on the ability to do the job?
2. When is the best time for a student teacher to begin teaching a complete load?
3. What are some alternative ways of getting the student teacher involved?

Assuming Increased Responsibility

Cooperative teaching is one of the key methods whereby a student teacher can assume responsibility immediately without being subjected to the consequences of failure. This arrangement allows both the supervisor and student teacher to share in guiding pupil learning. Pupils can observe that the supervising teacher and the student teacher are co-workers. Several types of joint activities can be selected which will achieve such a goal with little advance organization or planning. The following have been practiced by successful supervising teachers.

Cooperative planning
　　Teacher solicits ideas from the student teacher
　　Plans are jointly developed
　　Each reviews the plans of the other and offers suggestions
　　Resources are shared
Team teaching
　　Supervising teacher works with part of the class and the student teacher works with another section
　　Joint presentation
　　One teaching while the other assists
Sharing responsibilities
　　Records and reports
　　Lunch room, playground supervision, etc.
　　Directing homeroom activity

Assigning tasks that illustrate confidence in the student teacher
    Working with pupils who need assistance
    Performing tasks that demand special skills, e.g. operating equipment
    Presenting a new idea or concept
Attending faculty meetings and professional meetings

Responsibilities should be challenging to the student teacher. If assignments are mostly menial activities they may be interpreted as lack of faith in the student teacher's ability to perform more demanding tasks. This can affect self concept. Although routine tasks are a part of teaching, a student should be challenged with more demanding and more exciting teaching activities just as soon as they can be assumed.

A quick survey of the student teacher's activities can give an appraisal of progress toward initial adjustment to this new life. If the right proportion of responsibilities has been assumed by the end of the second week, a student teacher should:

Be independent in moving about the school
Know the names of the students
Have some professional knowledge about the pupils
Be able to make plans independently of the supervising teacher's direct instruction
Have taken some responsibility for teaching an entire class
Have met a number of other teachers and feel comfortable with them
Have observed teachers in other areas as well as in his major teaching area
Have enough confidence not to be dependent on the supervising teacher

It is not uncommon for a beginning student teacher to be extremely tired at the end of the day. Having been accustomed to a more passive role in the classroom, many student teachers become exhausted in executing their duties. The student teacher should not be overprotected, though, since fatigue is frequently part of a teacher's life.

Many supervising teachers wish to provide concrete requirements for a student teacher in order to insure that certain activities will have been completed. Worksheet Number Three in the Appendix is an adaption of one such list which was developed and used by a supervising teacher. It may serve as a point of departure for the teacher who wants to develop a statement of requirements and suggestions.

Case Study No. 9: AVOIDING TEACHING

Sherrill seemed to enjoy observing the classes that she was to take over. She even contributed to the supervising teacher's lessons by giving individual instruction when needed. On Friday of the first week, the supervising teacher asked Sherrill to bring in plans for her first lesson which was to be taught on the following Tuesday. She acknowledged the request, gathered her things, and left for the weekend. On Monday morning the supervising teacher received a message that Sherrill was sick and would not be in. She was absent on Tuesday and returned on Wednesday with no lessons prepared. Again she was told to prepare the lesson. She was absent the next two days. She returned on the following Monday but still was unprepared to teach. She shyly apologized for her absences and admitted that she felt that she could not get up in front of a group and teach. What should the supervising teacher do?

1. Insist that she make one more effort to write plans which would allow her to teach.
2. Give her further time for preparation.
3. Sit down with her and formulate plans for the first few lessons.
4. Reinforce her strengths and then help her begin teaching more gradually.
5. Consult with the university supervisor about the problem.
6. _____

Comment:

Although most student teachers are anxious to become involved in the classroom, an occasional beginner will be reluctant to do so. Generally the apprehension results from a lack of confidence which is reinforced by observing and by working with a supervising teacher who does so many things so well. Many supervising teachers have overcome such situations by involving the student teacher in activities which have minimum threat potential.

Questions:
1. Is this behavior so extreme that consideration should be given to withdrawing the person from student teaching?
2. What kinds of reinforcement techniques might help the student teacher to begin to accept more responsibility?
3. What kinds of teaching activities might produce less threat for a beginner?

Case Study No. 10: GETTING TO THE STUDENTS' LEVEL

After two weeks in the field, your student teacher expressed surprise at how little the pupils know and care. Her impatience with them shows frequently and she has commented to you that she cannot understand why they do not pay more attention. The main problem is that she is attempting to teach these young people by the lecture technique which was used in her college classes. What can you do to help her to make the balance of her experience more productive?

1. Plan a few sessions jointly.
2. Video tape a class and ask her to evaluate herself.
3. Teach a demonstration lesson which would indicate what is wrong with her teaching.
4. _____

Comment:
One of the most challenging tasks which a student teacher has to meet is that of adjusting to pupil level. A supervising teacher should see that the student teacher makes adjustments which will help her to better communicate with pupils. This probably dictates giving early attention to the problem and any of the above alternatives should be helpful. By all means something should be done or the situation will worsen.

Questions:
1. What is the best way to expose a student teacher to a variety of good techniques?
2. What procedures are helpful in assisting student teachers to understand the ability levels of their pupils?

Ten school days have passed. Brian Sims turns to his required student teaching journal and begins a summary of his first days as a student teacher.

"I feel a little tired right now. I do not think that I have worked so hard or been under as much mental strain in my life. This has been a hectic period, but it has been most beneficial.

"My supervising teacher is thoughtful and helpful. She has let me grade papers and kept me informed about all that was happening in the class. After each class she will answer my questions and we have talked about everything that seemed relevant.

"When I was introduced to the class, I spent the first few minutes telling the students about myself. In a few days I had assumed responsibility for teaching one group. I was surprised at myself the first day I taught. I was uneasy, but not like I thought I would be. As a matter of fact, I do not think I outwardly appeared to be nervous. Miss Bennett seems to have confidence in me, and this gives me more assurance.

"I find that I am busy most of the time. When I am not teaching I am usually talking with my supervisor or planning. I take work home most every evening. I have been to a faculty meeting, PTA meeting, and two ball games. No time to get bored."

Remember:

The student teacher must be approached with trust and confidence.

Emphasis should be placed on a team concept where two teachers work together.

Early activities should be planned so that the student teacher feels involved.

The most effective way of reducing student-teacher anxiety is to provide teaching experience.

Boredom sets in rapidly when the student teacher has nothing to do during the first few days of student teaching.

The early solution of small problems may prevent more complex problems later.

The student teacher is a beginner.

The student teacher should be allowed to assume teaching responsibilities gradually.

Involvement is imperative.

Every student teacher will be different.

USEFUL REFERENCES

BENNIE, WILLIAM A., **Supervising Clinical Experiences in the Classroom,** Harper and Row, New York, 1972, pp. 84-90.

DANZER, GERALD, "Student-Teaching Activities: The Spectrum of Possibilities," **Journal of Teacher Education** 22:4, pp. 483-486, Winter, 1971.

DYE, CHARLES, "Toward Effective Student Teaching" **Business Education World,** 53:21, 31, Jan.-Feb., 1973.

GRIFFIN, ALVIN D., "The Student Teacher Phobia," **Journal of Business Education** 52:214-16, February, 1977.

HORTON, LOWELL, **Role of the Classroom Clinical Supervisor,** Professional Improvement Series for Supervising Teachers, Northern Illinois University DeKalb, IL, 1979 (slide tape).

KERBER, JAMES E., and PROTHEROE, **Guiding Student Experiences in a Cooperative Structure,** Association of Teacher Educators, Washington, D.C., 1973.

LIMA, JUDITH, "A Student Teacher is Coming," **Business Education World** 53: 20-21, Jan.-Feb., 1973.

SEPERSON, MARVIN A., and JOYCE, BRUCE R., "Teaching Styles of Student Teachers as Related to Those of Their Cooperating Teachers," **Educational Leadership Research Supplement** 31:146-51, November, 1973.

Chapter Three

ESTABLISHING EFFECTIVE PERSONAL RELATIONSHIPS

Brian and Miss Bennett entered the teachers' lounge and almost collided with Gordon Rogers, a student teacher from Western who was completing his third week at Central City.

"I've had it," he fumed, as he made a quick exit. "That woman is impossible!"

Upon entering the room they found an exasperated Sally Hawkins, Gordon's supervising teacher, sitting alone at a table. Miss Bennett made a feeble attempt to ease the tension, but Ms. Hawkins only had the previous confrontation on her mind.

"I am thinking about calling Western and telling them that I can no longer tolerate this impudent snob."

"What is the problem, Sally?" inquired Miss Bennett. The response was more than she had anticipated.

"In the first place, he told me that he could be teaching effectively if I had taught the class better before he came. Imagine! This happened when I informed him that the pupils were not understanding his terminology. His plans consist of a few topic outlines, and he dashes them off after he gets to school in the morning. He hangs around with Mr. Reed most of his leisure time -- and he seems to find plenty of it. He just will not listen to me at all. I tell him what to do and how to do it and all he does is argue with me. If I had wanted my teaching criticized, I would have called the principal or supervisor. This young upstart is not the expert he thinks he is."

Miss Bennett and Brian exchanged glances but said nothing.

Miss Hawkins continued, "Furthermore, he has been making some immature comments which could have double meanings to the students. And two teachers have asked me not to let him observe them any more because of his behavior."

Miss Bennett interrupted with, "Have you discussed the problems with him or with his college supervisor?"

Miss Hawkins shook her head. "All our conferences end up in arguments. Just now I asked him to explain how two activities were related and he said, 'I don't need a cross-examination. I'm not stupid,' and stormed out. I thought I would wait until his supervisor visited again. What would you do?"

"I really don't know," responded Miss Bennett. "Fortunately Brian and I have been able to communicate very well."

Miss Hawkins looked at her, but said nothing. . .

EFFECTIVE PERSONAL RELATIONSHIPS: **More Than a Friendly Hello**

Student teachers believe that supervising teachers have more positive influence on their experiences than any other individuals. The reasons for this seem to focus primarily on the personal support given by supervisors. Apparently student teachers need empathy, understanding, and release from the pressures and anxieties of beginning teaching.[1] Supervising teachers are looked to for such emotional support.

Success in student teaching is contingent upon the relationship between the student teacher and supervising teacher.[2] A student teacher may possess adequate skill in methodology and be sufficiently knowledgeable in subject matter, but the experience is not considered to be a complete success if the relationship with the supervising teacher is less than desirable. A supervising teacher must give attention to establishing a supportive emotional climate. This begins by being willing to accept a student teacher in a professional atmosphere.[3]

The student teaching experience is a period of adjustment for both student teacher and supervising teacher. The student teacher is becoming familiar with a new environment and is testing skills in new activities. He is no longer a student but not yet a teacher, and this role confusion can lead to a great deal of uncertainty. It is apparent that the classes are the responsibility of the supervising teacher who will ultimately need to approve all actions. The student teacher's personality may be very much unlike that of the supervising teacher, and he may feel more comfortable with younger teachers or pupils.

The supervising teacher may feel pressured by many of the same conditions. The experience of having a student teacher in the room causes some teachers to feel so uncomfortable that it is a real task to share a class with a student teacher. Some supervising teachers have commented that they are uneasy when the student teacher shadows them all the time.

Although the conditions for tension exist, this very association has the exciting potential for wholesome and enriching contacts between an experienced educator and a teaching candidate. Differences in personality and style can add some zest to a class provided that not all energy is put into emphasizing the dissimilarities. The supervising teacher, being the more experienced, will normally be the first to recognize the dynamics of a situation and can take the initiative in establishing a constructive emotional climate.

[1] Ann Karmos and Carol Jacko, "The Role of Significant Others During the Student Teaching Experience," **Journal of Teacher Education** 28:5, p. 51, September-October, 1977.

[2] Ibid, p. 5.

[3] Arthur E. Garner, "The Cooperating Teacher and Human Relations," **Education** 92:99, November-December, 1971.

Creating Positive Relationships

A good relationship between a student teacher and a super-vising teacher develops as the following conditions become reality:

The student teacher is not to be a robot who copies the tech-niques of the supervising teacher.
The student teacher is accepted as a professional equal.
The student teacher is included in more than the immediate environment of the classroom.
The student teacher's ideas are encouraged, accepted, and implemented whenever possible.
The student teacher is treated as a person of authority in the presence of pupils.

Offering Suggestions in a Constructive Climate

Every supervising teacher will eventually be faced with the necessity of having to offer criticism or give advice to the stu-dent teacher. Many teachers wonder whether a direct approach can lead to a deterioration of relationships so that effective communication becomes more difficult. The attitude of the student teacher is often the clue to the selection of a desirable procedure. Too much preaching or dictating can lead to defensive reactions, but a student teacher may be just as concerned if there is a complete void in suggestions or reac-tions.

There is no single formula for creating ideal personal rela-tionships with a student teacher since personalities of real people are involved, but the following alternatives may be help-ful in producing an environment which is more tension-free:

Avoid criticizing the student teacher in the presence of others.
Criticism should be an attempt to uplift rather than to dis-courage.
Work together on a problem rather than criticize an individual's efforts.
Refrain from emotion-producing words or actions.

The supervising teacher must avoid being too critical. Con-stant censure is likely to cause a student teacher to resist or withdraw, thwarting progress toward the goal of self-evalua-tion. Since a student teacher almost never commits a blunder that is irreversible, extreme and continuous criticism seem unwarranted.

Personality Differences

It is difficult to be completely objective when personality differences exist because the problem rests with the feelings of the personnel who are involved. An atmosphere can develop where rigidity predominates. Some people find certain types of personalities abrasive and they have difficulty establishing effective communication with them. It can become very complicated when two such individuals are assigned to work together as student teacher and supervisor.

A little tension can be constructive provided it is acknowledged and accepted by both parties. There are certain moves which a supervising teacher can initiate which can improve such a situation:

Recognize and accept the differences.
Attempt alternative methods of communication which will place less emphasis on personality conflict.
Plan autonomous activities so that both have independent responsibility but the supervising teacher can still observe performance.
Arrange for the student teacher to have some time with other teachers with whom he can feel more comfortable.

How can a supervisor know whether personal relationships with a student teacher reach an acceptable level? Intuition can be misleading and student teachers may conceal their true feelings. In order to provide some criteria for objective self analysis, Worksheet Number Four was devised and appended in this book. Teachers who are interested in this type of self evaluation may wish to study it and adapt it for their use.

Case Study No. 11: SHE IS RUINING THE PROGRAM

Greg Martin was often selected as a supervising teacher because of his known teaching skill and popularity with students. He only accepted student teachers as a favor to those who needed an assignment in foreign language in his locality.

Monica Hart had been a difficult student teacher from the beginning. She was a sharp contrast to Greg in teaching style. Her presentations were unexciting, students were bored, and discipline problems were beginning to occur. Monica responded with detentions, additional homework assignments, and expulsions from class.

Students are beginning to complain. Although Greg supports the student teacher, the pupils still refuse to accept her. Now they are refusing to enroll in advanced foreign language study for next year because of their dissatisfaction with Monica and fear that they would have another student teacher like her. If enrollment declines his position is in jeopardy. It is time for action. What should he do?

1. Resume control of the class and ask the student to observe a while longer and note the differences in technique.
2. Team teach with the student teacher.
3. Discuss the situation candidly with Monica and present a list of specific improvements which need to be made.
4. Urge the students to be patient and remind them that the student teacher will only be in charge for a brief period of time.
5. Seek a transfer for the student teacher.
6. _____

Comment:

When student teachers become negative they may be projecting their feelings of insecurity. This can be complicated when teaching in the shadow of a popular teacher. The problem could be approached by increasing a student teacher's options for presenting an exciting lesson. The teacher might spend more time talking with the student and sharing ideas for making the lessons exciting. It might be beneficial to video-tape the student so she can observe how she appears to the group.

Questions:

1. Does conflict with pupils possibly imply some conflict with the supervising teacher?
2. What particular difficulties exist for a student teacher who is working with a very popular instructor?

3. How can a teacher accept a student teacher whose performance is minimal at best?

Case Study No. 12: THE STUDENT TEACHER IDENTIFIES CLOSELY WITH ANOTHER TEACHER

Gary had appeared uncomfortable with you from the beginning, and he seemed to be ill-at-ease in his contacts with several other teachers. He did develop a close relationship with one of the young teachers in the building. They seemed to have a lot in common and you observed that your student teacher appeared to be avoiding you in order to be with the other teacher. There is evidence also that he has been talking over his problems with this teacher.

Since you feel that a closer communication needs to be developed between you and Gary, what course of action do you pursue?

1. Inform the student teacher that the two of you need to spend more time together in conference.
2. Take steps to arrange for specific times when the two of you are together both formally and informally.
3. Ignore the situation.
4. Talk to the other teacher and explain the problem which seems to be developing.
5. _____

Comment:

There may be several reasons for the student teacher to be associating with another teacher, but it is rather obvious that he is uncomfortable with the supervising teacher. The younger teacher is more likely to share his interests, accept his values, and be less critical because he does not have to accept the responsibility for Gary's progress. The supervising teacher should attempt to develop a more comfortable relationship with the student teacher.

Questions:

1. What should a teacher do if he discovers that a student teacher thinks that he is too busy to talk with him?

2. What are some clues that a teacher might be treating a student teacher in a condescending manner?
3. What might prompt a student teacher to become close to another teacher?

Case Study No. 13: A REVEALING LUNCHROOM CONVERSATION

You are standing in the cafeteria line when you hear someone talking loudly about a person who is old, set in her ways, never lets a student teacher try new things, etc. When you take a quick glance toward the voice, you see your student teacher conversing with another teacher. She does not mention you by name, but you are sure that you are the person referred to in the conversation. What do you do?

1. Dismiss the incident as that of a self-conscious girl who has found a willing listener.
2. Remind her that such comments are unethical.
3. Do not mention the conversation but indicate that you saw her talking with the teacher at lunch.
4. Have a very candid discussion with her.
5. _____

Comment:
Criticism such as this can be an attempt to place the blame for inadequacy on someone else. The essence of this situation is that the student teacher is experiencing problems. It appears that a bit more flexibility on the part of the teacher may be in order. Remember that informal conversations are often merely catharsis and the actual situation may be quite exaggerated. This observation may be verified in the teachers' lounge.

Questions:
1. Based on the above incident, what could be some basic differences between the student teacher and supervising teacher?
2. How could a supervising teacher lead this student to a discussion of the differences between them?

EFFECTIVE PERSONAL ADJUSTMENT: **Up One Day: Down the Next**

There is a relationship between self-concept and student teacher performance. Garvey[4] found that seniors who rated high in student teaching also reported high self concepts. It seems to confirm the notion that success in student teaching is affected by self-concept.

Another investigator[5] found that students experienced feelings of success and satisfaction from those activities which involved them in active, personal relationships with . . . pupils in the classroom. The criterion of success frequently used by student teachers was the amount of personal satisfaction the experience provided rather than the achievement of instructional objectives. It is very important for student teachers to discover that teaching offers opportunities for personal satisfaction, and the nature of the relationship between supervising teacher and student teacher has a direct bearing on realization of that goal. If the student teacher is forced to expend energy maintaining, improving, or clarifying this relationship, there may be little enthusiasm or energy left for the larger task.

Self concept is undoubtedly affected by the extreme importance which is placed on success in student teaching. It may be further complicated by the fact that student teaching is a new experience which calls for a series of adjustments. This newness can initiate an emotional cycle which runs from elation to dejection. This innovation cycle seems to be typical of any new experience. It involves different levels of emotional reaction at various stages in the period of development involved. A typical eight-week student teaching experience will possibly produce emotions ranging from elation to depression.[6]

[4]Reba Garvey, "Self-Concepts and Success in Student Teaching," **Journal of Teacher Education** 21:3, pp. 357-361, Fall 1970.

[5]Malcom A. Lowther, "Successful and Unsuccessful Experiences of Student Teachers in Secondary Education," **Contemporary Education** 41:6, pp. 272-275, May, 1970.

[6]Donald M. Sharpe, **A Brief Guide to Secondary Student Teaching,** Indiana State University, Terre Haute, Indiana, 1970, p. 11.

WEEKS

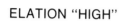

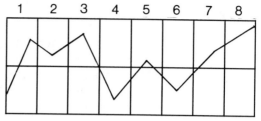

ELATION "HIGH"

DEPRESSION "LOW"

The student will most likely enter the experience with feelings of insecurity and fear. These initial concerns are soon overcome as he is welcomed by the staff and finds that the pupils are human after all. The peak of enthusiasm may be reached after a few days as a student teacher. Typically, a rather sharp decline to a state of depression will occur in about the third or fourth week. This may be caused by such factors as an altercation with a pupil, poor grades on the first test he gives, or a criticism by the supervising teacher. After this low, there should be a gradual building of confidence and satisfaction up to the conclusion of the experience.

Supervising teachers frequently observe changes in feelings which have resulted from some personal situation or from a recent experience. The above illustration may explain why. The supervising teacher is in a position to influence feelings and modify behavior if there is an awareness of the student teacher's feelings. If a supervisor is aware that elation and dejection are normal phenomena, he can better help the student teacher cope with such feelings.

Many worries are eliminated or diminished through normal student teaching. However, the supervising teacher must be prepared to assist the student teacher in reducing or managing anxiety. It is important that the supervising teacher recognize that the student teacher is a human being whose new surroundings are creating new problems and restructuring old ones. These personal matters will be reflected in the day-by-day relations with the supervising teacher and will affect his approach to the pupils and to teaching.

Case Study No. 14: A STUDENT TEACHER WANTS TO QUIT

Jim walked into class early one morning and found that someone had put glue in all of the woodworking vises and tightened them. When you walked in, Jim was muttering and obviously angry. He vowed that when his student teaching stint was over he would never again set foot inside a classroom. What should a supervisor do in this situation?

1. Tell him to pry them apart and continue as if nothing unusual has happened.
2. Tell him that such behavior communicates that a teacher is really alienating his pupils and examine what can be done to prevent this from happening again.
3. Tell him that an incident like this probably will never happen again.
4. Comment that they at least were working with tools for a change and then dismiss the incident as if it is not too critical.
5. _____

Comment:

Behavior which seems to be pointed at a student teacher can create an intense feeling of anger and depression. The problem may be that a student teacher may take the incident as a personal affront instead of displaced aggression, which it might well be. The supervisor has to be able to help a student teacher understand the context of the act, including the reasons why it happened, before the surface feeling can be discussed.

Questions:

1. Should a supervising teacher intervene at this point and try to determine who was responsible for the act?
2. Should a supervising teacher be concerned that a student teacher reacts so negatively to this incident?

Case Study No. 15: PAUL FAILS TO REACH OUT

Paul tried to be as inconspicuous as possible. He was alone as much as he could be and, when he was with others, he had nothing to say. He did not even appear to be listening when there was conversation. His voice projection was low in the classroom and he hardly looked up when he spoke. His performance was similar in conferences. Obviously he is too shy to become an effective teacher unless he changes.

What do you do in this situation?
1. Suggest that he consider some career other than teaching.
2. Attempt to build his confidence by placing him in situations where he can succeed.
3. Tell him that he will have to sink or swim and force him into challenging situations.
4. Attempt to discover the reasons for his timidity and then work on a possible solution.
5. Discuss the situation with the pupils and encourage their assistance in helping him overcome his feelings of timidity.
6. _____

Comment:

Behavior of this type, especially during the early days of student teaching, occurs more frequently than one might assume. Withdrawal seems to be the way some people cope with a new situation. In spite of his apparent fears there is something which has attracted this individual to consider teaching.

Questions:
1. Is there some condition which may be causing him to withdraw?
2. Are there some activities which even a timid person can perform?
3. What kinds of relationships help a person to overcome his withdrawal tendencies?
4. Should he be recommended for a teaching certificate if this pattern of behavior continues?

Case Study No. 16: THE STUDENT TEACHER WHO IS TOO WELL-ADJUSTED

You have put a lot of effort into making Susie's student teaching experience happy and successful. You apparently succeeded too well. She has had no real difficulties and she is convinced that everything about teaching is marvelous. She is really anticipating next year and you have reason to believe that she thinks that it will be as simple and exciting as student teaching. At this point you begin to wonder if you have not overprotected her and begin to question whether you have really been fair to her.

What course of action do you now take?
1. Do nothing, assuming that her idealism will provide a better frame of reference for any teaching situation.
2. Try to arrange for some experiences which confront her with some of the problems of teaching.
3. Describe the unrealistic aspects of her student teaching experience and explain what she might logically have to face next year.
4. Arrange for her to observe some troublesome classes in the school.
5. Arrange for her to talk with some beginning teachers.
6. _____

Comment:
The student teacher has somehow managed to avoid any problems. This could indicate that she is being protected. Since problems are often the grist whch produces growth, it would appear that the student teacher should be involved in a broader segment of the educational program.

Questions:
1. What kinds of problems present real learning opportunities?
2. Is it better to present a glowing picture of teaching rather than to look at some of the more unpleasant realities?
3. Can student teaching actually be very realistic?

EFFECTIVE PERSONAL RELATIONSHIPS WITH PUPILS: **The View from the Other Side of the Desk**

Socially the student teacher may be only a few days away from college life. A student teacher may appear at the school looking like a teacher, but this appearance does not guarantee that behavior is going to show any more maturity. Initially, he is merely a college student who is dressed up, painfully aware that some of the pupils are not much younger than he is. High school students may appear larger than he had remembered and more sophisticated than he had assumed. A sea of restless elementary pupils may be quite unsettling to a person who has not recently seen so many children together. The pupils call him a teacher, the university personnel regard him as a student, and the supervising teacher may consider him as a teacher one moment and a student the next.

The problem of adjusting to students frequently presents a real dilemma for the inexperienced student teacher. Motivated by the desire to be accepted but admonished to get the respect of pupils, he may find himself vacillating from one position to the other or wavering just enough to be inconsistent. Perhaps the greatest error is in trying to role play a different personality.

The initial classroom stance assumed by the student teacher is determined more by a concern for survival than by a desire to direct an exciting, interesting, or informative class. In an attempt to become established, a student teacher may concentrate so much on safe subject matter and traditional instructional techniques that he becomes oblivious to students. If this occurs initially, the pupils may respond negatively and complain about dull classes. Very little will happen in the classroom until the student teacher makes some gesture which indicates a genuine concern for students.

The student teacher may also be tempted to assume a role which has been found to be effective in achieving acceptance in other situations. This is usually a predicament involving peer acceptance in which there is a completely different relationship than is appropriate in student teaching. The social techniques which have worked in college are often the ones that will cause problems with pupils. The result may be that there is a breakdown in respect for the student teacher as an adult. Often an intense desire to be accepted causes rejection.

Occasionally a student teacher will attempt the hard line approach in which rules are set down and privileges are suspended until pupils have proved that they are willing to obey. Theoretically standards are then relaxed and more tolerance prevails. The problem is that he will probably be too insecure to be either convincing or authoritative and become entangled in a web of unrealistic demands and rules which cannot be enforced.

The task of the supervising teacher is to help the student teacher develop a more comprehensive outlook in the area of pupil-teacher relationships in the school environment. The following procedures are worthy of consideration in assisting the student teacher.

Arrange for the student teacher to assume complete responsibility gradually.

Try to identify any unusual behavioral patterns and counsel with the student teacher before any unfortunate moves are made.

Point out that pupils want their teacher to act like an adult.

Stress that genuine respect from a class is achieved from such factors as enthusiasm, respect for people, and interesting class sessions.

Help the student teacher understand students and their life styles.

Arrange case studies of two or three of the more unique students in the class.

Out-of-class contacts also present occasional difficulties. It is not uncommon for a beginning student teacher to wonder if discipline will deteriorate if he speaks to pupils when they meet out of class. Male student teachers in high schools frequently receive attention from teen-age girls and may be tempted to see them socially. An insecure or immature student teacher may gravitate to the company of pupils, avoiding more uncomfortable contacts with teachers. At times a student teacher may innocently become the victim of an amorous member of the opposite sex in such innocent-sounding requests as being asked for extraclass assistance, to be taken home after an evening meeting, or even in the innocuous act of sitting by a student.

The alert supervising teacher will be aware of this possibility and will attempt to provide a satisfactory set of guidelines for the student teacher's informal contacts with pupils. The student teacher may need to become aware of potential problem situations and learn techniques for achieving satisfactory solutions. It should be kept in mind that he will be very conscious of the supervisor's approach and may make decisions on the basis of that example.

It is sometimes difficult to convince student teachers that they can affect pupil behavior in the classroom. If such is the problem, Worksheet Number Five in the Appendix may be useful for a student teacher to use in analyzing teacher impact upon pupils. The form which should be completed by the student teacher calls for evidence of having met acceptable criteria in establishing good personal relationships with pupils. It further challenges the student teacher to consider ways of improving personal behavior in the classroom.

Case Study No. 17: THE STUDENTS CALL ME CAROL

Your student teacher has been attempting to establish rapport with the pupils by displaying a genuine friendliness with them. She has generally been successful and the pupils seem to enjoy their contacts with her. All went well until some of the students discovered that her first name was Carol. A few of them have taken the liberty of calling her by her first name. Carol is concerned now because she realizes that pupils do not address teachers by their first names and she fears that this may lead to a deterioration of respect for her. She asks for your advice about what to do.

What course of action do you take?

1. Talk with the pupils involved and request that they accord her the respect due a teacher.
2. Suggest that she explain that they can best support her as a friend if they do not ask for the liberty of a first-name approach.
3. Tell her to firmly inform them that her name is Miss Smith.
4. Suggest that she ignore the pupils whenever possible.
5. _____

Comment:

Student teachers sometimes feel that rapport has deteriorated when pupils call them by their first names. The tendency seems to be to overreact. Perhaps the teacher's first task is to help Carol analyze why students have addressed her by her first name and discuss whether it really makes any difference. The conversation may develop into a discussion of how friendly relationships can be developed while respect is still maintained. Carol's task will be to inform the students how she wants them to refer to her and still retain their respect.

Questions:

1. How can a situation such as this one be prevented?

2. What are some methods of establishing rapport with pupils which can be used by student teachers?
3. What prompts pupils to use the first name of a teacher?

Case Study No. 18: "YOU ARE ONLY A STUDENT TEACHER"

Your student teacher was in the room alone with the class when he made an assignment which a few of the students did not like. He explained that it was required and would be counted as part of the grade. The pupils countered with, "I don't believe that; you are only a student teacher. Miss Haynes is the teacher and she will give grades." Your student teacher again stated the requirements and continued with the class, but was very upset by the challenge. He asks for your advice.

What do you do?
1. Support him in what he did.
2. Talk to the class and define the student teacher's role clearly.
3. Indicate that he must prove that he is the teacher by his actions.
4. Talk privately with the pupils involved.
5. _____

Comment:
Student teaching has been considered to be analogous to cooking in someone else's kitchen. Regardless of the autonomy given, there will be an occasional skeptic who will attempt to enhance his position by calling attention to the fact that the student teacher is in a subordinate role. Unfortunately the student teacher may actually feel that he is not totally in charge and may respond accordingly. The supervising teacher should probably first support the student teacher. However, the supervisor should also make certain that both parties understand the amount of responsibility that the student teacher can exercise.

Questions:
1. How can a supervising teacher help a student teacher gain the confidence of the class?

2. Are there any responses which student teachers can be prepared to give skeptics?
3. What are the most difficult teaching roles for student teachers to assume?

Case Study No. 19: TOO CLOSE FOR COMFORT

Pam's student teaching had been going well, so the supervising teacher was exercising only minimal supervision. After several weeks, the supervising teacher observed that certain pupils were constantly surrounding her. When asked if the students were a nuisance, Pam responded negatively and then stated that the pupils had been to her apartment a few times and that she felt that she was really getting to learn about high school students. Since the supervisor had given Pam considerable latitude and had not observed her too closely, this was a surprise. Upon learning that this informal contact exists but aware that the student teacher is doing well, should the supervising teacher take any action?

1. Reprimand Pam for her unprofessional behavior.
2. Tell her it was a good idea to learn more about students.
3. Explain the importance of maintaining rapport with pupils, but stress that it is not a good idea to become too close to students.
4. _____

Comment:
The student teaching process is a difficult one for the student teacher. It is a time of change -- in status, attitude, and even in professional goals. It is a time that needs strong guidance in order to create success in teaching. The student teacher is still a student, yet is on the verge of becoming a career professional. During this time she may still be playing both roles, but it is important that she move toward the more mature roles. This case study would suggest that some immaturity exists. An alert supervising teacher will help a student teacher to establish desirable student contacts without becoming involved in informal situations which might cause problems.

Questions:
1. Should a supervising teacher become involved in after-school activities between a student teacher and her pupils?
2. What guidelines are useful in counseling student teachers about pupil-teacher relationships?

Case Study No. 20: THE STUDENT TEACHER INVITES A FEMALE STUDENT TO A SOCIAL FUNCTION

Jay is a personable individual who has been the center of attention from a clique of girls since he started his student teaching. One girl became very friendly with your student teacher and he obviously was enjoying it. They talked frequently during the day and the girl often came by after school. Extracurricular activities sometimes brought them together in the evenings. One day your student teacher tells you that he would like to invite her to be his date at a party he plans to attend in another community. He asks for your opinion.

What do you tell him?
1. Indicate that his personal life is no concern of yours.
2. Describe the possible professional implications.
3. Project the possible deterioration in student rapport if certain pupils learn that he has dated one of their peers.
4. Approve a date of non-school locations, but discourage any such behavior at school functions.
5. _____

Comment:
It is difficult to separate a social life from a professional life in some of the more innocuous-appearing activities. This problem can be compounded when the age span between the two people is relatively slight. The key question in this case seems to be whether a teacher can conduct a dual relationship with a student and still be accepted as a teacher.

Questions:
1. How do student teachers get closely

involved with students?
2. Can a social life be completely separated from a professional life?

Case Study No. 21: CONFLICT BETWEEN THE STUDENT TEACHER AND THE CLASS

Your student teacher had never liked the seventh-hour class. The conflict between them had been developing for several days and it came to direct confrontation with a test review. A defensive explanation of a questionable test item led to an angry response from several pupils. The student teacher failed in an attempt to shout them down. You pass by the door and observe that he is in trouble.

What course of action do you take?
1. Walk quietly into the classroom but make no immediate gesture to the class.
2. Demand that the class get quiet.
3. Take over the class and discuss the problem.
4. Walk on by and do nothing until you have a chance to talk with the student teacher.
5. _____

Comment:
If the situation has become a shouting match, the supervisor will probably need to intervene. Any action taken must have the benefit of the pupils in mind. It might be good to begin to see what caused the confrontation.

Questions:
1. What can cause hostility between a student teacher and the class?
2. What is the supervising teacher's role in reconciling the differences?
3. What preventive alternatives could be considered?

Brian and Miss Bennett walked toward the lunch room and were stopped for a moment by a student who had a question about a homework assignment. Brian was still aware of the incident they had witnessed earlier between Gordon Rogers and Sally Hawkins.
"Pardon me if I seem impertinent," Brian began, "but I am glad that I have you as my supervising teacher instead of some others I have seen."

"You are good natured enough to work with almost anyone, Brian," countered Miss Bennett. *"But this business of human relationships is frequently overlooked. If either party becomes defensive, I can see where some real problems can develop."*

"We have not always agreed on everything, but I've always felt that you respected me. And even when I took exception to some of your ideas, you were tolerant," commented Brian, *"and you certainly have made me aware of how important it is to be a human being as well as a teacher. That is one of the most valuable lessons I have learned."*

As they turned into the cafeteria, Miss Bennett dismissed the praise by remarking, *"One thing that we have always agreed on is the quality of food in the cafeteria. It has a way of creating consensus among people who generally disagree on most things."*

They picked up a wet tray and nodded toward the chili in preference to the hot dogs supreme.

Remember:

A good example is better than a thousand words in personal relationships.

Student teaching is a growth situation in personal relationships for both students and teachers.

A student teacher cannot make maximum development when treated in a condescending manner.

The student teacher is a colleague though an inexperienced one.

Differences in personalities should be considered as an asset instead of treated as a problem.

Honesty, thoughtfulness, and tact affirm and help to establish and maintain good personal relationships.

Student teaching is generally considered to modify the personality of a student teacher toward a more positive self concept.

USEFUL REFERENCES

BERG, ROBERT, **Helping Develop a Trusting Relationship in a Clinical Setting,** Professional Improvement Series for Supervising Teachers, College of Education, Northern Illinois University, DeKalb, IL. 1979 (slide tape)

BRAND, MANNY, "Student Teaching: The Emotional Cycle," **Music Educators Journal** 65:54-55, October 1978.

CAMPBELL, LLOYD, and WILLIAMSON, JOHN A., "Practical Problems in the Student Teacher Cooperative Teacher Relationships," **Education** 94: 168-9, November, 1973.

CASEY, JOHN, and McNEIL, KEITH, "Attitudinal Dimensions of Supervising Teachers and of Elementary and Secondary Student Teachers," **Journal of Teacher Education** 23:3, pp. 358-362, Fall, 1972.

CRUICKSHANK, DONALD R., and KENNEDY, JOHN J., "The Role of Significant Others During the Student Teaching Experience," **Journal of Teacher Education** 28:51-5, September-October, 1977.

DAVIS, JON K. and DAVIS, KATHRYN W., "Maximizing Positive Student Teaching Supervising Relationships Through Performance Contracting," **College Student Journal** 11:193-6, Summer, 1977.

GAZDA, GEORGE, **Human Relations Development,** Allyn and Bacon, New York, 1973.

GUERRIERI, DONALD, "Student Teaching - A Team Concept," **The Balance Sheet** 57:300-2, 332, April, 1976.

JAX, JUDY A., **Home Economics Education Handbook: Teacher Trainer Program,** 1976, ERIC ED 135 934.

JOHNSON, JAMES, "The Student Teacher as Self: or How Am I Doing," **Kappa Delta Pi Record** 13:70-2, 94, February, 1977.

KARMOS, ANN, and JACKO, CAROL M., "The Role of Significant Others During the Student Teaching Experience," **Journal of Teacher Education** 28:5, pp. 51-55, September-October, 1977.

LIPKE, BARBARA S., "Give Your Student Teachers a Break," **Journal of Teacher Education** 30:31-34, March-April, 1979.

LOUISIANA STATE UNIVERSITY, **Changes in Self-Concept During the Student Teaching Experience,** Research Report Vol. 2:5, Louisiana State University. Nov. 1972, 9 pp. ERIC ED 074 055.

LOWTHER, MALCOM A., "Successful and Unsuccessful Experiences of Student Teachers in Secondary Education," **Contemporary Education** 41:272-275, May, 1979.

MORRIS, JOHN E., and MORRIS, GENEVA W., "Stress in Student Teaching," **Action in Teacher Education** 2:4, pp. 57-61, Fall, 1980.

MULLENNEX, JOHN M., **A Study of a Training in Helping Relationships Experience for Cooperating Secondary School Teachers and Its Effects Upon Selected Perceptions of the Teachers and Their Student Teachers,** 1973, 13 pp. ERIC ED 088 792.

PETERS, WILLIAM H., **An Investigation of the Influence of Cooperating Teachers in Shaping the Attitudes of Student Teachers Toward the Teaching of English,** 1971, 14 pp. ERIC ED 074 052.

PIERCY, FRED, and OHANESIAN, DEBORAH L., "Assertive Training in Teacher Education," **The Humanist Educator** 15:41-46, September, 1976.

TRAUGH, CECELIA E., and TILFORD, MICHAEL, "Student Teaching and Its Influence Upon 'Student-Centeredness' and 'Subject-Centeredness,' " **The Teacher Educator** 14:3, pp. 28-32, Winter, 1978-79.

Chapter Four

WORKING WITH COLLEGE SUPERVISORS

The morning session had just started and Brian was beginning his introduction to a new unit of study. It had been difficult to find the right approach and he was uncertain whether the activities would move smoothly. He looked up just in time to see the door open and watched a familiar figure move to a back seat. He forced a smile and tried to conceal his apprehension. Not his college supervisor today! What will he think of this class? Why couldn't he have come yesterday when the lesson went so well?

Miss Bennett whispered a word of greeting to Dr. Douglas and handed him a copy of Brian's plan. She then excused herself from the class, assuming that Brian might be more comfortable if there were only one supervisor in the room. Dr. Douglas indicated that they would confer after the class was over.

A few minutes after the class had ended, Dr. Douglas entered Miss Bennett's office for a conference. He talked informally for a while, and then opened his folder to his notes and began to inquire about Brian's progress. . .

THE COLLEGE SUPERVISOR: **Professor; Liaison; Consultant**

The college supervisor occupies a unique role among all professionals. He works primarily in the public schools but is not a member of the staff; he is a college instructor who may not teach in the traditional sense. He is frequently called upon to be an ombudsman charged with reconciling differences between parties involved in student teaching.

The teaching role of the college supervisor is manifest through individualized instruction. In some cases such instruction is as simple as the presentation of ideas and concepts to a student teacher. In many cases it becomes more complex and is involved with the attempt to help a student teacher develop through instructional analysis and feedback. In this case a college supervisor may observe a student teacher and sometimes additionally record the teaching act on an analysis form or on an electronic device. The procedure will conclude with a conference where ideas are suggested for change or improvement. The college supervisor is an instructor in a classic sense and his availability to work with student teachers in this manner should not be underestimated.

The personnel in the cooperating schools may consider the college supervisor to be a facilitator of the student teaching experience. Because of this fact, his actions may be more responsive to professional need instead of administrative demand. His strengths may rest with the fact that he must use persuasion rather than coercion.

Many supervisors have found that teachers and pupils consider a college supervisor to be an evaluator and cooperate to see that a good image of the student teacher is presented. This unwritten pact assumes that the college supervisor will penalize the student teacher for having difficulties if revealed. On the other hand a student teacher may hesitate to complain because of a fear that a college supervisor could cause the situation to worsen. It is even no surprise to learn that the pupils were more cooperative during a supervisory visit than they are in the normal course of events. College supervisors need the cooperation of the school personnel if they are to perform a productive role.

The college supervisor's role is a complex one involving several activities and responsibilities. The supervisor is frequently regarded only as a liaison person who interprets the university program to the cooperating school and explains the cooperating school's program to the appropriate personnel at the university. As an intermediary the college supervisor attempts to eliminate misunderstandings or to resolve conflicts between the supervising teacher and the student teacher. Public relations may consume a considerable amount of a college supervisor's time. The position requires close contact with school administrators in order to promote and sustain good relations between the school and the university. He is also a university representative in contacts with other school personnel.

The most preferred role is that of clinical supervisor where the college supervisor actually works with a student teacher to improve instruction. In this way he becomes involved with the student teacher in analyzing pressing problems and developing solutions. Drawing upon his background and experiences, the college supervisor facilitates the improvement of teaching through the supervisory process. The college supervisor should obviously be involved in helping the student teacher with his work. He has been described as a guide, confidant, and trouble shooter whose availability and knowledge of teaching can be very beneficial to the student teacher. If a candidate has a particular problem, the supervisor may be in the best position to provide assistance.

The typical college supervisor is also a part-time administrator. This role involves the process of interviewing and assigning student teachers and seeing that university and state requirements are being adhered to. On occasion a college supervisor must interpret policy as it applies to a particular situation. More specifically an effective supervisor will be involved in the following kinds of activities:

Interviews candidates for student teaching and recommends assignments
> Makes judgments about the type of assignment needed
> Searches for school settings which can provide the experience needed

Orients student teachers to their assignments
> Explains requirements
> Interprets forms
> Makes suggestions concerning the initial school visit
> Alerts student teachers to the necessity of adapting to the school and community

Acquaints supervising teachers with their responsibilities
> Interprets the college student teaching program and requirements
> Shares unique information about the student teacher
> Helps determine the schedule for the student teacher
> Suggests desirable types of activities

Counsels with the student teachers concerning problems
Assists student teachers in development of instructional techniques
> Observes student teachers' classes, studies their written work, and confers with them
> Helps in the development of teaching skills

Helps student teachers learn to evaluate themselves
Helps supervising teachers evaluate their student teachers
Leads seminars with student teachers

A study by Elsmere and Daunt[1] revealed that student teachers and supervising teachers consider the contacts made by the college supervisor an important factor in the student teaching program. Students seemed to want and need support from someone from the university.

The college supervisor also represents the education profession. He may have had recent experience as a teacher or been in contact with many public schools in his role with the university. Through this professional experience and

[1]Robert T. Elsmere and Patrick Daunt, **Effects of the Size of the Student Teacher Group on the Supervisory Program,** The Association of Teacher Educators -- Indiana Unit, Research Bulletin No. 1, 1975, Ball State University, Muncie, IN, p. 18.

knowledge of educational trends and innovations, he should possess a broad knowledge of educational developments. The college supervisor should not be overlooked as a resource person who can serve as a helpful consultant on curricular, instructional, and organizational matters.

Case Study No. 22: THE STUDENT TEACHER BECOMES ANXIOUS ABOUT THE COLLEGE SUPERVISOR'S VISIT

"I know I should not be so worried but I just get scared when I think about his coming. I am sure that I will become frightened when he walks into the classroom."

The above statement was made by your student teacher. His teaching progress seems to be satisfactory and there is no apparent reason for him to have a fear of the college supervisor, but he is quite anxious about any visits from university personnel. What do you do to attempt to help this situation?

1. Tell him that he will get over his fears by simply teaching as he had planned.
2. Inform the supervisor before the observation so that he will understand the student teacher's feelings.
3. Cover for the student teacher when the college supervisor visits and then explain the anxiety that exists about being observed.
4. Arrange to have some other teachers observe so the student teacher can become more accustomed to having another person visit his class.
5. _____

Comment:

The expression seems to represent a fear of being observed that is quite frequent among preservice as well as inservice teachers. One logical explanation for this anxiety is that an observer is often perceived to be judging the performer. If the supervising teacher can convince the student teacher that a college supervisor can be a helper, then the student teacher may view the visit differently.

Questions:
1. Why do some persons have a fear of being observed while some seem to have no reluctance at all?
2. How can a supervising teacher communicate to the college supervisor that a student teacher is reluctant to be observed?
3. Can a supervising teacher help a student teacher feel less threatened by a college supervisor's visit?

ASSISTING THE STUDENT TEACHER: Big Daddy or Big Brother?

The college supervisor's principal mission is to assist the student teacher in developing teaching competency. Since each student teacher will reveal a different pattern of needs and abilities, the college supervisor must determine the type of assistance which is needed and then use knowledge, skill, and resources to help the student teacher. In order to expend the best effort the college supervisor will need to know the student teacher and be acquainted with the teaching situation. This will necessitate spending time in the classroom and in conference with the student teacher and the supervising teacher.

The college supervisor encourages the student teacher to go beyond superficial appraisal of teaching into a more intellectual approach, to think about what is happening, to see relationships, and to formulate plans of action for subsequent experiences. The college supervisor can be a catalyst who causes the student teacher to formulate a broader perspective on teaching through reflection on the current experience.

Many universities include a seminar as part of the professional experience. This encounter provides an opportunity for college supervisors to see their student teachers in a different environment and to deal with the immediate concerns of student teaching. The well-structured meeting can provide a situation where the candidates for teaching may compare notes, ask questions, and formulate conclusions through interaction with their peers. The college supervisor uses the seminar to answer questions and to guide the dialogue into analysis of problems where alternatives for teaching practice may be considered.

The teacher center concept has created a new role for many college supervisors. In the past, the supervisor has been viewed by almost everyone as an evaluator or critic of student teachers. Some of these new arrangements now permit a supervisor to actually demonstrate the processes which he advocates for the student teacher.[2]

The college supervisor who can serve as a model of good teaching will more likely be considered to be a person who can offer assistance to a teaching candidate. In one instance a supervisor was confronted by a student teacher who was having difficulty understanding suggestions for change of technique. Arrangements were made with the classroom teacher and the college supervisor taught the class showing the student teacher what should be done. The student teacher made a marked improvement during the next few weeks.[3]

The college supervisor frequently has difficulty gaining the complete confidence of the student teacher in spite of his most sincere efforts. It is a problem for the student teacher to avoid the feelings of being judged and having to defend every action. A college supervisor has to establish rapport and the supervising teacher can help by demonstrating confidence in the college supervisor.

The college supervisor attempts to render assistance to the student teacher in various ways. The typical types of activities are the ones indicated below:

Gives personal assistance
    Answers questions concerning requirements and details
    Counsels when problems exist
Works in the development of teaching skills
    Attempts to help the student teacher develop competency
       in various teaching situations
    Calls attention to teaching resources and ideas
    Observes and analyzes classes with student teachers
Serves as an intermediary in disputes or misunderstandings
    between the student teacher and the supervising teacher
Helps the student teacher evaluate his performance and goals
Serves as a teacher on a one-to-one basis

[2]James E. Kerber and Donald W. Protheroe, **Guiding Student Teaching Experiences in a Cooperative Structure,** ATE Bulletin 33, 1973, p. 22.

[3]James E. Higgins, "I See and I Remember -- The University Supervisor As a Demonstrator," **The Teacher Educator** 9:2, Winter, 1973-74, pp. 8-10.

Case Study No. 23: THE STUDENT TEACHER REJECTS THE SUGGESTIONS OF THE COLLEGE SUPERVISOR

The college supervisor spent several hours visiting your student teacher's classes and conferring with each of you. His primary concern appeared to be to help Jeri improve in some of her weaker areas and his suggestions offered alternatives which could lead to better performance. She became upset and said that the college representative had been too critical of her. Her final comment was, "How can he make any valid judgments? He wasn't here long enough to know what this class is like."

Since you recognize some validity in the supervisor's suggestions, what moves do you make?

1. Appear non-committal hoping that this action will create confidence for a more objective analysis at a later time.
2. State that you feel that the suggestions have merit and encourage the student teacher to follow the recommendations.
3. Analyze the suggestions and determine their validity in a context which the student teacher might understand.
4. Arrange for a demonstration which would illustrate the supervisor's suggestions.
5. _____

Comment:

It would appear that no growth will occur if the comments are summarily rejected. Perhaps much of the problem with teaching today is that teachers reject ideas and continue their routines without any analysis.

Questions:

1. How valid is the comment that the supervisor only viewed a brief part of class?
2. How can a supervising teacher establish better communication between student teacher and college supervisor?
3. How do you help a student teacher overcome the feeling of being threatened?
4. Should the supervising teacher attempt to agree with one or the other or adopt a non-committal course of action?

Case Study No. 24: A CONFLICT BETWEEN A STUDENT TEACHER AND HER COLLEGE SUPERVISOR ABOUT THE TEACHING OF VALUES

Ann's college supervisor observed her on the day that she chose to use a popular film that was designed to show value conflicts. During the critique he complimented her on technique and timing but suggested that she could have gone further in getting students involved in sharing what it was like to be in a conflict situation. When he mentioned that she might have students role play the conflicts and then discuss the basic issues, Ann resisted saying that the students were too young for such intense situations. Her supervisor disagreed and the conference ended without any reconciliation of the different points of view.

What do you do?
1. Ignore the situation.
2. Take a position which you feel is right and then counsel with Ann.
3. Talk with Ann and see if there are some actions which she can take which will be acceptable to her supervisor.
4. Share your concern with the college supervisor.
5. _____

Comment:
The conflict nature of this incident conceals the fact that a teacher is attempting to defend her actions. A student teacher may feel that it is her role to perform for the supervisor and when her practices are questioned she may look for an excuse. The main problem may be that she misunderstands the role of a college supervisor.

Questions:
1. How can a supervising teacher help a student teacher overcome a fear of a college supervisor?
2. What should a supervising teacher do if a college supervisor suggests different alternatives and procedures?
3. What are some guidelines for having student teachers deal with value topics?

ASSISTING THE SUPERVISING TEACHER: **A Relationship of Peers**

Both supervising teacher and college supervisor bring knowledge and insight into the student teaching situation. The supervising teacher possesses knowledge of the school and pupils; the college supervisor provides an increased understanding of the student teacher and the responsibilities of student teaching. Both parties can benefit if they work together. An initial function of the college supervisor is to acquaint the supervising teacher with the nature of the university student teaching program and to help a teacher to understand the supervisor's role.

Prior to, or early in the student teaching experience, the college supervisor and supervising teacher will probably consider the following topics:

The basic rationale of the student teaching program
    Philosophy
    Underlying principles
    Objectives of student teaching
The college and state requirements
    Number of hours to be taught
    Observation requirements
    Forms which are to be completed
    Reports and due dates
    Attendance requirements
    Types of activities
    Conferences
    Plans
    Competencies to be achieved
    Evaluation and grading
Information about the student teacher
    Academic record
    Personal information
    Particular qualities
    Potential difficulties
Basic concepts of supervision
Role of the teacher education institution

It is beneficial for the college supervisor to be informed of the general nature of the school in order to be aware of the particular challenges or opportunities facing the student teacher. The following information is helpful for a college supervisor:

The general profile of the class or classes
The general nature of the content which the student teacher
  will teach
Established routines and procedures
Special projects or activities
General teaching procedure utilized
Available resource materials

The next contact with the college supervisor will probably occur a few weeks later. During this time the college supervisor will likely observe the student teacher in a classroom setting and conduct an extensive conference in regard to the experience. He will solicit the supervising teacher's analysis through a private conversation if possible. After being apprised of the current situation, the college supervisor may assist the supervising teacher by:

Suggesting additional experiences for the student teacher
Summarizing the student teacher's progress from a different
  perspective
Suggesting alternative procedures in methods, planning, con-
  ferences and pupil contacts
Reviewing requirements and seeing that the university stan-
  dards and state regulations are met
Counseling student teachers who are having problems
Serving as a liaison person between the student teacher and
  supervising teacher

The visit of the college supervisor may present an opportunity to utilize professional talents for the benefit of the specific teaching environment. Knowledge and information may be provided in regard to such areas as:

Latest developments in educational programs
Teaching skills
Resource materials
New techniques of instruction
Information about the college and teaching programs

The college supervisor's peer relationship will go beyond communication with the cooperating teacher. A college supervisor should establish working relationships with others in the building. A discussion with the principal about requirements and policies should help to establish the necessary conditions for a good student teaching experience. They may want to explore the advantages of a student teacher's being in the building and to agree on the new responsibilities of the parties involved.

Other teachers have an impact upon student teachers and they should also get to know the college supervisor. Teaching aides and other assisting personnel should be introduced to the college supervisor. The mutual exchange of views and ideas from these contacts can be beneficial and informative for all concerned.

Case Study No. 25: THE COLLEGE SUPERVISOR EXPRESSES A POINT OF VIEW WHICH IS CONTRARY TO THE SUPERVISING TEACHER'S POLICY

In the course of your discussion with the college supervisor he makes some statements concerning educational practice which conflict with your views. He then asks questions in regard to your intended procedures in working with the student teacher. You tend to feel rather strongly that you are correct and that you should follow the procedure as you had originally planned. How do you respond to his questions?

1. Explain your point of view and indicate your intent to proceed as you had planned.
2. Attempt to resolve the differences through discussion.
3. Conceal your view but proceed as you wish.
4. Follow his recommendations.
5. Explain the difference to the student teacher and permit him to decide.
6. _____

Comment:
A professional relationship should allow an open, frank exchange of views and ideas. The conflict between the ivory tower and the world of reality is constantly discussed and debated. This case study seems to illustrate the fact that universities and public schools have differing ideas concerning what should happen in education. One would assume that all parties would best be served if the differences were identified and openly discussed.

Questions:
1. What are some differences that might exist between college supervisor and supervising teacher?
2. For the student teacher's sake, who should prevail?

The conference with the college supervisor developed easily. Dr. Douglas asked questions which assessed the nature of the student teacher's progress in meeting requirements. He was particularly interested in the amount of responsibility the student teacher was assuming, and he suggested a few teaching procedures which might be tried. He answered Miss Bennett's questions and discussed a few ideas about evaluation that might be used for more effective analysis of Brian's teaching.

Brian came by after he had completed some commitments. After a discussion of his progress, Brian and Dr. Douglas explored plans for future goals and tasks. Dr. Douglas suggested that planning should be more thorough and that Brian should spend a little more time observing other teachers and concentrating on the analysis of the moves that seemed to make them successful. In response to one of Brian's questions, Dr. Douglas presented a rather detailed explanation of the technique of reflection through written records and analysis. Brian took out a pen and scribbled a few notes in the margin of his lesson plan and made a few entries in his student teaching journal. Miss Bennett silently mused over the change in Brian's reaction to his college supervisor.

Remember:

The college supervisor possesses expertise which is valuable to both supervising teacher and student teacher.

The college supervisor is in a position to assist with problems and difficulties.

The college supervisor is concerned with the improvement of educational practice.

The supervising teacher should consult with the college supervisor.

The college supervisor facilitates and supplements good supervision.

The college supervisor needs the cooperation of supervising teachers and student teachers.

The college supervisor is a guide, confidant, and troubleshooter.

The college supervisor should be informed of the student teacher's activities in detail.

The student teacher will perform better when the college supervisor takes an active role in his experiences.

USEFUL REFERENCES

BENNIE, WILLIAM A., **Supervising Clinical Experiences in the Classroom,** Harper and Row, 1972, pp. 72-80.

BIBERSTINE, RICHARD, "The University Supervisor: A Variable in Teacher Preparation," **The Teacher Educator** 11:4, pp. 23-27, Spring, 1976.

CREAMER, GLYNN N., "The College Supervisor of Secondary Student Teaching in State and Private Schools," **Contemporary Education** 46:4, pp. 249-252, Summer, 1975.

DIEM, RICHARD A., and SCHWITZ, JAMES E., "The Instructional Alliance in Student Teaching," **Contemporary Education** 49:72-4, Winter, 1978.

ELSMERE, ROBERT, and DAUNT, PATRICK, **Effects of the Size of Student Group on the Supervisor Program,** Indiana Association of Teacher Educators, Research Bulletin No. 1, 1975, 58 pp.

FRENZEL, N. J., "Perceptions of University Supervisors," **The Teacher Educator** 12:4, pp. 14-17, Spring, 1977.

HIGGINS, JAMES E., "I See and I Remember -- The University Supervisor as a Demonstrator," **The Teacher Educator** 9:2, pp. 8-10, Winter, 1973-74.

_____ , "The Trouble with Harry," **Contemporary Education** 47:4, pp. 241-243, Summer, 1976.

JACKO, CAROL M., and KARMOS, ANN H., "The University Supervisor: What Place in Academe?" **The Teacher Educator** 14:1, pp. 21-24, Summer, 1978.

LANG, DUAINE C., QUICK, ALAN F., and JOHNSON, JAMES A., **A Partnership for the Supervision of Student Teachers,** The Great Lakes Publishing Company, Mount Pleasant, MI, 1975, pp. 26-28.

LANG, ROBERT, "Role of the University Clinical Supervisor," **Professional Improvement Series for Supervising Teachers,** Northern Illinois University, DeKalb, IL. (Slide tape)

McDANIEL, THOMAS R., "To My Student Teachers: Reflections on Teaching By a College Supervisor," **The Teacher Educator** 12:3, pp. 7-9, Winter, 1976-77.

MORRIS, JUNE ROSE, "The Effects of the University Supervisor on the Performance and Adjustment of Student Teachers," **The Journal of Educational Research** 67:8, pp. 358-362, April, 1974.

NEREZ, ANNE, "The Roles of the University Supervisor: Perceived Importance and Practical Implications," **Foreign Language Annals** 12:471-75, December, 1979.

PATTY, AUSTIN, "Classroom Teachers Will Replace College Supervisors," **Contemporary Education** 44:3, pp. 179-183, January, 1973.

PEASE, DAVID W., "Quis Custodet Custodes?" **The Teacher Educator** 12:1, Summer, 1976, pp. 26-30.

Chapter Five

SUPERVISING OBSERVATIONS

Brian entered Miss Bennett's room and happily announced that he had just completed his final observation. Miss Bennett was somewhat surprised and quickly responded, "But you still have four weeks left in student teaching. Are you certain you have completed all of them?"

"Oh yes, I have been keeping record," explained Brian. "I started early and observed frequently so that I could get them over with. What a relief! The teachers I observed are all right, but I get bored just sitting in a classroom."

Miss Bennett protested mildly, "But there is value in observing. Are you certain you want to finish just yet?"

Brian's answer was definite. "I learn more when I am teaching than I do when I am observing. I wish the university would be more practical and dispense with some of its 'Mickey Mouse' requirements. Now I can devote my time to teaching. If you want me to assume some additional work, let me know. I have time for it now that observations are out of the way."

Miss Bennett, who was not quite prepared for this candid appraisal of observations, started to reply when the warning bell sounded signaling that class was due to begin in five minutes. This was beneficial in a way because she was not certain that she could respond to Brian's feelings at this moment. Now she would have the opportunity to find out more about observations before she gave a response...

OBSERVATIONS: Learning By Looking

A colorful sports personality is credited with the nonsensical aphorism that you can observe a lot by looking. This bit of whimsy says in a delightful way what professionals know: observation is an acceptable, productive way to learn. The universality of observation experiences as part of teacher education programs attests to the support which the teaching profession gives for this process. Any student teacher should expect to round out the experience by completing a number of observations.

Observation is a practical way of introducing student teachers to practitioners who possess differing skills and techniques. The learner's world is broadened through these contacts because so many different kinds of situations can be viewed in a relatively brief period of time. It is through this process that a future teacher can be aware of sophisticated teaching techniques without having to discover them through trial and error in the classroom.

An observation should be part of the process of self discovery where a student teacher engages in self-analysis in order to determine needs and to compare skills with others. Observations should also broaden a student teacher's perspective through increased awareness of teaching styles and techniques.

It is often a paradox that a student may tend to resist observations because of a feeling of inadequacy. A student teacher may feel a need to demonstrate how to teach rather than to learn about it. The supervising teacher must convince such a student teacher that it is productive to check ideas and techniques with the skills of others.

A student teacher who observes periodically should realize that teaching competence is not dictated by a model, dominated by a particular personality type, guaranteed by the mastery of subject matter, or insured by being able to capture student interest. According to one expert these are the ingredients of successful teaching but do not necessarily equal successful teaching.[1] If a student teacher can grasp this concept, a significant stride in professional development will have been made. Observations will become more worthwhile when the various components are synthesized into a personal style.

A student teacher should observe teachers who vary in styles and skills in order to become acquainted with a wide range of procedures. In addition, it is desirable to schedule observations in classes which are in fields other than the student teacher's major. The college years have led to subject specialization and isolation from other areas. Observations should serve to expand a student teacher's perspective of school curricula. Based on this experience, it is logical to assume that the teaching candidate will examine more carefully how other activities mesh with those in his chosen field.

The logical observation sequence will begin in the supervising teacher's classroom with a student observing the supervising teacher. The teacher may use this occasion to provide information or to illustrate techniques. Many teachers have found demonstrations have worked when several explanations have failed.

It is essential to include teachers with varying degrees of skill in an observation schedule. Good teachers can be models of inspiration and challenge for the beginner because the atmosphere is enriching and challenging. However, a student teacher who observes only polished and experienced teachers

[1]Gerald A. Danzer, "Student Teaching Activities: The Spectrum of Possibilities," **Journal of Teacher Education** 22:4, p. 482, Winter, 1971.

may fail to gain perspective about teaching and this could lead to feelings of inadequacy. For this reason it is advisable to include observations of some inexperienced or less effective teachers so that a student teacher can see pedagogy in perspective. The critique and analysis of such teachers must be done tactfully, but the effort is worthwhile when it can be shown that teachers do influence the classroom climate.

Observations should be active exciting experiences. A student teacher will likely have a more positive attitude toward observations if they provide answers to some questions about teaching. The challenge is to provide productive observation experiences for student teachers. If so, observations will be given higher priority in scheduling.

Case Study No. 26: A FEW QUESTIONS AND AN ABUNDANCE OF CRITICISM

Your student teacher comes in the first day and sits down to observe. She writes down all that you say and do. On the second day, she wants to know why you set up the reading groups the way you did and why the children write at the beginning of the class. It is not long until the "whys" are beginning to get to you. It seems she is questioning everything you do. She has even stated that your methods are not the ones she learned in college. She appears unusually critical as if she thinks she knows better. What course of action should you take?

1. Sit down with her and answer all her questions concerning the reasons for your methodology.
2. Contact her college supervisor and question whether the assignment should be continued.
3. Ask her to teach a particular concept alone in order that you may discover her teaching skill.
4. _____

Comment:

The student teacher may have a narrow concept of the reasons for observations. It appears that the ploy is to learn by being critical. Perhaps it is a means of disguising her feelings of inadequacy. Obviously a little patience is needed but there is also a need for the student to understand her role as an observer. It might be beneficial to give her a checklist to complete instead of permitting her to randomly criticize what she sees.

Questions:
1. What would be some reasons for criticizing the reading sessions?
2. How can a teacher take the initiative without offending the student teacher?
3. Should student teachers feel free to examine the practices of their supervising teachers?

THE OBSERVATION SEQUENCE: **One Step Leads to Another**

Observations should begin at the onset of student teaching and continue until the end of the experience. The needed input varies considerably from week to week and so observations must be matched with the readiness of the student teacher.

Initial Observations

Initial observations should fulfill the objective of having the teaching candidate become familiar with the teaching environment. This involves getting to know the pupils and becoming aware of the classroom routine. A student teacher will want to know what the pupils are like, how the teacher functions, how routine procedures are managed, and how a new person will fit into the whole classroom scheme. A supervising teacher should concentrate on the following topics and see that the student teacher is becoming aware of their significance:

Management techniques and classroom routine
Awareness of the supervising teacher's style
Classroom climate and pupil behavior patterns
Knowledge of content and method
The problems of teaching
Instructional materials used in the classroom

The outcome of these structured observations should be an orientation to teaching with an understanding of the dynamics of the classroom and of the personnel who are involved in it. It should further help to determine initial behavior patterns.

The initial days may also see the student teacher becoming aware of the school setting. There may be requests to observe other teachers in the student teacher's major area or those who have similar classrooms. This should provide a more complete picture of the immediate environment as well as alleviate any boredom that might result from extensive observation of a supervising teacher. The initial observations should raise the level of interest of student teachers by stimulating and challenging them to become involved. They should lead to familiarization with the classroom and role awareness.

Developmental Observations

After the objectives of the initial observations are achieved, new demands begin to confront the student teacher. As previously indicated a student teacher will be gradually increasing teaching activity from the first day in the school. As this involvement becomes more intense a new set of teaching tasks will develop. These experiences may lead to the realization of what is needed in order to know more about teaching and students.

Observations can provide assistance in both areas. After a few days a student teacher may find it beneficial to visit other teachers in order to discover other styles and techniques. The following components may be viewed and analyzed with some degree of effectiveness:

Learn additional teaching techniques
    Techniques of arousing student interest
    Identify skills which the student teacher can use
    Learn what makes good teaching effective
    Analyze teaching behavior
Gain a more comprehensive understanding of students
    Compare the same student in different school situations
    Study the forces that determine student behavior
Identify teaching needs
    Needs of the student teacher
    Needs of the pupils

The developmental observations which will encompass a considerable portion of a student teaching experience should expand a student teacher's knowledge of teaching skills. During this time the teaching candidate will be analyzing and discovering areas of strength and weakness. A supervising teacher will need to continue to review and discuss observations with the student teacher. This dialogue should cause a student to reconstruct the experience and gain insights which may have been overlooked previously.

Culminating Observations

The final observations can potentially be the most rewarding of all because the student teacher will have a more comprehensive outlook on teaching. The student teacher now should view teaching in more scientific terms and have a better understanding of the critical role of the teacher in directing learning.

This more sophisticated period should allow the student teacher to become more evaluative with the ability to detect relationships which would have been overlooked earlier and to understand why a teacher is behaving in a particular way. In addition, the student teacher may be considering alternatives which would work in his situation or which could be adapted to a different setting. This rewarding time should help the student teacher acquire a broader perspective of teaching.

An example of a sophisticated analysis of teaching through observation was provided by a student teacher who consciously observed both good and poor practices. His strength was that he converted all generalizations into positive suggestions when he recorded them. This resulted in a list of positive qualities which could be reviewed for his own benefit at a later time. In one such class, he made the following comments:

Allow students to answer the question posed without interrupting
Discuss directions to tests and question the students in order to determine whether the directions have been understood
If a threat is made, a teacher should be able to carry it out
Be patient and tolerant

It will not matter long whether a poor, average, or superior bit of teaching was observed. He has compiled a list of principles in a positive tone which will guide his teaching.

The final observations will likely be concerned with the following:

Providing a more comprehensive background for analyzing ideas and practices
Learning to evaluate teaching
    Determining basic principles associated with teaching
    Recognizing theoretical implications
    Formulating a valid concept of what constitutes effective teaching

Gaining a more comprehensive picture of the function of the school

    Other grade levels and other subjects taught

    Learning experiences which have preceded the student teacher's grade level

    Experiences which will follow the student teacher's grade level

    Relationship of various content areas to one another

    Curricula in the school, including experimental programs

A student teacher should have formulated a more comprehensive outlook on teaching as the experience nears its completion date. Education may be viewed in a more integrated way which means understanding better the critical role of a teacher. Observation at this time will cause a student teacher to achieve a better perception of good teaching.

If a student teacher fails to observe at any phase of his experience, a valuable learning opportunity will have been missed. If observations are crammed into any brief period of time, a student teacher will be denied an opportunity to learn as completely as possible. The student teacher's concept of what to look for may be vague at all three levels of the experience unless the supervising teacher provides some direction.

Observations In Other Schools

In addition to the vertical concept of observation, the horizontal domain must be recognized as part of a total sequence. Many profitable observations can be made outside the building where student teaching is completed. A nearby school, for example, may operate on a different scheduling pattern or serve a different type of student population.

Student teachers often are eager to see some special programs or different facilities, such as special education clinics or diagnostic centers. Since student teachers frequently teach at only one grade level, it can be profitable for them to see younger and older students in order to formulate a more complete picture of the development of curricula. Combine this with a few incidental contacts and impressions, and there emerges a valuable activity in having students observe in other school settings.

Case Study No. 27: I WOULD PREFER TO TEACH

The pupils accepted Patti as their teacher from the beginning. Since she was needed in a class which had individualized instruction, it was easy to defer her observations of other teachers. When you approached her concerning the observation requirements, she commented that all the observation she needed was the chance to watch the children grow as she taught them. It is tempting to yield to this request, but you also feel that observations can be beneficial.

What do you do?
1. Indicate that she can improve her teaching through selected observation of other teachers.
2. Specify that university requirements have to be met.
3. Ask some teachers to invite her to observe.
4. Assign one specific observation and ask her to see if she still feels the same way.
5. _____

Comment:
The satisfaction of working with children can cause other requirements to seem insignificant. However, the isolation of a classroom may present a more limited concept of what teaching is about especially if a student teacher is working in a unique environment. Observations should be broadening so that greater perspective is secured. Perhaps a particular instructional concern could be identified and Patti could observe to seek an answer.

Questions:
1. What should Patti be looking for that she cannot learn in her own classroom?
2. What is the difference between observing while working and the traditional practice of giving complete attention to a class?

Case Study No. 28: THE STUDENT TEACHER CRITICIZES A TEACHER HE OBSERVES

Steve has just observed a teacher who is regarded as somewhat ineffective. He greets you with the comment that it was the worst class he has ever seen and criticizes the teacher's procedure. You suspect that most of his comments are accurate, but you wonder how you can approach the discussion of the observation and still remain ethical.

What course of action do you pursue?
1. Confess that you wanted him to see the class in order to see what he had viewed and then admonish him to keep his thoughts confidential.
2. Analyze the points mentioned in detail so that he can objectively appraise the class from a valid frame of reference.
3. Caution him not to be too quick in making judgments.
4. Ask him what he would have done if he had been the teacher in that situation.
5. _____

Comment:

The analysis of this situation extends beyond the matter of teaching technique. A student teacher should see the whole spectrum in order to see what learning is like, but one questions the ethics of characterizing another teacher as a poor example of professional practice. In any event a teacher should direct a student teacher to formulate positive concepts from this activity.

Questions:
1. How can you assess the validity of the student teacher's remarks?
2. What would you want a student teacher to learn from observation of a poor teaching performance?
3. Would a discussion prior to the observation have been helpful?

SCHEDULING AND FOLLOW THROUGH: **Precision Should Prevail**

In a sense an observation begins with the arrangement for the visit. The student teacher who makes arrangements in advance can expect more from the observation than the one who simply walks into a class to observe. The observation time may be spent more efficiently since this procedure gives a teacher an opportunity to structure the class so that it has more relevance to the observer. It allows a teacher to plan to make learning features more discernible and reduces the probability that the student teacher will spend most of the time observing a test or study session.

Arrangements for observations may be made by the student teacher, supervising teacher, department chairperson, or building administrator. The student teacher should learn the procedure which is practiced at his school and then follow that policy. Some schools operate on an informal basis while others require that specific requests be made. A useful student teacher visitation request form is included in the Appendix as Worksheet Number Six. Teachers may wish to use this form or a modification of it for scheduling observations.

Once the observation is arranged, a frame of reference can be developed which will make the observation more valid. Student teachers seem to profit most from those observations when they are concentrating on specifics. A student teacher who realizes that it is important to note a teacher's style of interrogation, for example, will gain more from the experience than the one who is only instructed to observe to discover what can be learned. A supervising teacher should apprise a student teacher of the style of the teacher to be observed, if possible. Sometimes the supervising teacher may simply want the student teacher to compare the performance of one or more pupils in a different class.

The student teacher should arrive for the observation early enough to allow for any preliminary discussion or orientation which the teacher desires to make. A student teacher can take more meaningful note of the classroom procedure if he is aware of what is planned. Early arrival also insures that the normal flow of activity will not be interrupted.

The teacher will undoubtedly take note of the observer's reactions from time to time. Thus, the student teacher should be cued to display an active interest in the class rather than to appear bored or indifferent. The observer should show a genuine interest in the work of the class. Teacher observation may seem trivial unless a student teacher believes that it can be beneficial. The anecdotal records in nearly every college student teaching office contain examples of a student teacher who went to sleep while observing or appeared so bored that the teacher asked the supervising teacher not to permit any more classroom visits. An alert supervisor will see that a student teacher knows what to look for and understands how to get the most from each visit.

An observation is not completed with the conclusion of a

lesson. The observer should make a point to thank the teacher for allowing a visit to the class. The teacher may want to make a few comments about the lesson or even solicit the observer's reactions to what was seen. A few constructive comments by the student teacher are always in order. The teacher who watches a student teacher hastily making an exit following an observation may be aggravated or disappointed. The student teacher's reactions to a class can affect a teacher's receptiveness to further observations.

The experience of an observation concludes with an analysis session between the supervising teacher and the student teacher. This discussion can lead to a very productive examination of teaching. Questions are good techniques for encouraging the student teacher to reflect on what was observed.

Many student teachers and supervising teachers prefer to have a set of objective criteria which may be detected during an observation. Those who prefer such instructions will find two excellent checklists as Worksheets Number Seven and Eight in the Appendix.

The results of the observation should be manifest in the student teacher's performance. If the observation resulted in learning, improved teaching should result. Actual modification of teaching following an observation will depend upon the attitude of the observer, timing of the observation, development of observational criteria, and application of what has been learned to the observer's own specific teaching situation. An observation can often be more beneficial than a similar period of teaching.

The supervising teacher's responsibilities for observations are concurrent with those of the student teacher and a team approach is called for. The supervising teacher should be directly involved in helping the student teacher learn from observation experiences. Generally, the responsibilities are summarized as follows:

Set up the process for outside observations
    Arrange a tentative pattern of observations
    Assist the student teacher in scheduling observations
Prepare the student teacher for the observation
    Describe the dynamics of the situation to be observed
    Indicate what might be learned in the class
Arrange for observations which fit the student teacher's particular readiness

Provide for observation of various types of teaching situations
   Academically talented classes and less gifted groups
   Different types of educational programs within the school
   Teachers with differing styles of teaching
Help the student teacher analyze and evaluate what was observed
   Discuss significant activities
   Determine what was learned

Case Study No. 29: NOTHING CHANGES

   Since you were convinced that it would be beneficial for Gregg to observe other classes, you scheduled visitations which you thought would be profitable. Although he apparently was completing the suggested observations, there was no evidence that he was gaining any ideas from what he was seeing. Your inquiries about the nature of other situations brought only vague responses and a rather indifferent attitude regarding the teaching styles of the other teachers. Furthermore, there has been no evidence of his having changed his teaching as a result of visitations. Since you are concerned about this, what course of action do you take?

1. Suggest that he discontinue observations for a few days.
2. Structure the observations so that he will know what to look for.
3. Cue the teacher to discuss the class with him.
4. Ask the student teacher to take notes on the observation or to write a brief summary of his visit.
5. Conduct a follow-up conference on the observation.
6. Attempt to arrange the next few observations with the most interesting teachers you can find.
7. _____

Comment:
   The lack of any kind of response may result from the fact that Gregg saw no reason for completing the observation. It might be a good idea to think about what has occurred prior to the observation. If there was little orientation it might be well to begin there. The terminal inquiry could also be examined to see if the questions contribute to a

student teacher's understanding or whether they may appear to be an oral examination. In any event, the observations ought to be continued.

Questions:

1. What causes an individual to be a bored observer?
2. What causes one to observe a situation with considerable interest?
3. Why would a student teacher be reluctant to talk about a class which he has observed?

Brian entered the teachers' work room with a list of notes and a look of enthusiasm on his face. He had just come from an observation of one of the more popular teachers in the building.

"That class of Mr. Lawton's is everything you said it was. I really enjoyed watching him teach. I picked up two or three ideas that I can use next week in my class. Time went by so quickly that I had difficulty realizing that I had been there for an hour. He even had me involved in the discussion."

Miss Bennett resisted the temptation to remind him of his previous critical attitude toward observations and simply commented, "I thought you would enjoy seeing him. Now, what did you notice about the way he aroused student interest?"

Remember:

The supervising teacher should guide the student teacher in choosing observations.

Observation is the most efficient method of learning about teaching in many situations.

Observations will be more meaningful if adequate preparation is made.

An observation will be worthwhile in proportion to the analysis provided at its conclusion.

Observations can provide opportunities for reflection on the nature of one's own teaching.

The perceptive observer will improve professional skills.

USEFUL REFERENCES

BARNETT, JEFF, "Learning Through Observation," **Professional Improvement Series for Supervising Teachers.** Northern Illinois University, DeKalb, IL. (Slide/tape)

CLOTHIER, GRANT, and KINGSLEY, ELIZABETH, **Enriching Student Teaching Relationships (Supervising Teacher Edition),** Midwest Educational Training and Research Organization, Shawnee Mission, KS pp. 6-7.

DANZER, GERALD A., "Student-Teaching Activities: The Spectrum of Possibilities," **Journal of Teacher Education** 22:4, pp. 481-483, Winter, 1971.

DREYFUS, AMOS, and COHEN, HADARAH, "Enhancing Student Teachers' Analytical Perception of Science Lessons," **Science Education** 63: 363-71, July, 1979.

KENNEDY, EDWARD, "Peer Observer," **Journal of Physical Education and Recreation** 49:56, September, 1978.

LANG, DUAINE C., QUICK, ALAN F., and JOHNSON, JAMES, A., **A Partnership for the Supervision of Student Teachers,** The Great Lakes Publishing Company, Mt. Pleasant, MI, 1975, Chapter 6.

MUELLER, DORIS L., "Observing Student Teachers in a Competency-based Program," **Peabody Journal of Education** 53:248-53, July, 1976.

SIEDENTOP, DARYL, **Teacher Assessment in Physical Education,** September, 1977, ERIC ED 152 702.

SMITH, SARA DAWN, "Taking a Closer Look," **The Teacher Educator** 14:1, pp. 2-9, Summer, 1978.

Chapter Six

HELPING THE STUDENT TEACHER PLAN

Brian seemed to be gaining confidence daily as he became acquainted with the school routine and participated in more teaching activities. His work with the class had been satisfactory, and he was scheduled to assume a full teaching load within a few days. He had been working diligently on lesson plans and was seen poring over a college textbook and consulting the planning section of his student teaching guide.

Miss Bennett assumed that Brian would consult with her about his teaching ideas, but he had not made any reference to his plans since she assigned a unit to him. She wanted to see his tentative plans in order to be certain that he was making progress, and she wondered how much suggestion she should make once she did see the ideas that he was developing.

Miss Bennett decided to approach the subject with her student teacher. At the beginning of their conference she casually stated, "Four more days and you will have full responsibility for the class. Do you have your ideas worked out?"

Brian shuffled some papers and looked at her in an uncertain manner and shook his head . . .

REQUIRED PLANS: **Valuable Tools or Busy Work?**

Student teachers sometimes have difficulty understanding the importance of planning. The plans which have been constructed in college courses were probably centered upon hypothetical teaching situations which may have stressed form more than content or utility. The broad concept of planning is easy to overlook.

A supervising teacher may be confronted with the task of explaining the role of planning and its effect on teaching. Perhaps a review of the basic dimensions of planning would be in order. The student teacher should be aware of the fact that plans constitute more than arranging to have something to do every minute of the period. Consider discussion of the following questions in looking at the total concept of planning:

What is to be taught?
    Content
Why should it be taught?
    Goals and objectives
When is it to be taught?
    Timing and sequencing

How will it be taught?
  Methods and techniques
Who will be taught?
  Nature of the student group
How will it be evaluated?
  Accountability

The above framework provides for considerable flexibility while showing how various components of a lesson are related. It should prevent the student teacher from feeling consumed by useless paper work and present planning as a viable tool instead of a mechanical procedure.

The supervising teacher has the right to expect a student teacher to prepare both long-range and daily plans but must help the student teacher learn to prepare, especially in the early phases of teaching. Planning should be required which will achieve the following results:

The student teacher will be a partner in the teaching-learning process.
The planning process will be an experience which is designed to assist in thinking through objectives and deciding which teaching techniques will best meet those objectives.
The plan will provide security in working with a class.
The plan will serve as a guide to insure effective learning.
The plan will offer the supervising teacher an opportunity to make suggestions before a class is taught.
The completed plan will be a guide which can be used in the analysis of a lesson.

Successful planning involves a much larger scope than that ordinarily envisioned by a student teacher. Competency in planning involves the ability to do long-range organization as well as daily scheduling. Any successful student teacher should demonstrate the ability to develop a long-range plan. Advance planning encourages the student to effectively organize and to consider a whole design rather than just a daily combination of segments. Such planning can help the student teacher to schedule more activities on a daily basis and give more time to provide the best lesson possible.

The behavioral objectives concept is a planning dimension that can be quite helpful to students. This procedure allows a student teacher to define desired pupil behavior, to schedule activities which will lead to the development of such behavior and to define the criteria which determines whether it was met.

Such an activity can lead to the realization that planning and execution are much more closely related than may have been assumed.

A supervising teacher should encourage a student teacher to experiment with various types of planning in order to determine the values of each and to eventually develop a comfortable style. In order to facilitate the development of working plans, some agreement will be necessary concerning the form and detail of plans as well as the schedule for their completion.

It is reasonable to assume that a student teacher will need assistance in developing a planning procedure that is suitable. A supervising teacher can be of help by reviewing the tentative plans, asking questions, and offering occasional suggestions. If such assistance is effective, student teachers will recognize that good plans are the best tools which teachers can have for teaching effectively.

Case Study No. 30: NO ALLOWANCE FOR IN-VIDUALS

Rene's lesson plan was presented in advance and was explained thoroughly. The only flaw was that she had made no provision for the fact that some of the brighter pupils will finish their assignments quickly while most of the students will still be working. If the class is taught as proposed, some of Rene's pupils will have nothing to do while the others are completing their work. This has happened before and it appears that she is having some problem providing for individual differences. What do you do to help her?

1. Nothing. She will soon discover the reason and correct it.
2. Inform her that the plan will not work and ask her to redesign it.
3. Discuss the plan with her step by step and analyze what is likely to happen.
4. _____

Comment:

A supervising teacher assists a student teacher in developing planning skills. The plans are submitted in advance so that the supervising teacher can detect weaknesses or offer suggestions which would improve learning. The student teacher needs to be made aware of the fact that pupils work at different rates.

Questions:
1. How can the concept of individualization be interpreted to a novice who is struggling with preparation?
2. What parts of a lesson plan need attention for individualization?
3. How can a teacher discuss inadequate plans with a student teacher and refrain from being too dominant?

Case Study No. 31: THE STUDENT TEACHER PRESENTS NO WRITTEN PLANS

Reed is a confident student teacher. He had not produced any written plans in spite of your frequent requests. His teaching has been acceptable, but you are aware that it could be improved if you could talk with him in advance about his proposed procedures. On Monday morning you ask him if he has his plans for the week. He casually remarks that he does not write anything down because it is all in his mind. Since you feel that analysis is important, what do you do to get written plans?

1. Indicate that you will cease to ask for plans when he demonstrates that he can teach well.
2. Allow him to discover the need for planning by permitting him to teach when he is not prepared.
3. Refuse to let him teach until the required plans are produced.
4. Critique his lessons and indicate where he could have done better if he had planned more thoroughly.
5. Ask the college supervisor to clarify the university position in regard to required lesson plans.
6. _____

Comment:
Two options seem worthy of consideration: 1) Even when the student teacher's plans are adequate, it can be productive to discuss ideas together in order to enrich the lesson, and 2) if the planning is not as thorough as desired, the

teacher is obligated to do all that he can to insure the best instruction possible. Both of these options would involve analyzing the plan before the lesson is taught, and a written plan would contribute to such analysis.

Questions:
1. What causes resistance to written plans?
2. What are some key points which a supervising teacher could make to a student teacher like Reed?

Case Study No. 32: CONSIDERING THE POOR LESSON PLAN

Your student teacher has just submitted his plan for the next class and it is apparent that it will not be effective. Since you realize its limitations and your student teacher does not, what course of action do you pursue?

1. Wait until he teaches the class and then discuss the reasons for lack of success.
2. Confer in advance and help him devise a better plan.
3. Be prepared to assist the student teacher when he teaches the class.
4. _____

Comment:
Many persons learn from mistakes, but positive attitudes are more likely to develop through success. In spite of the former contention, it appears that better learning will result if there is consultation which will in turn produce a better lesson plan. The successful class would then serve to reinforce the idea of having a well-developed plan.

Questions:
1. What alternatives are available to a supervising teacher who wants to discuss a poor lesson plan with his student teacher?
2. Is it better for a student teacher to experience frustration before the nature of planning is discussed?

ADVANCE PLANNING: **One Week or One Hour?**

It is frequently a problem for student teachers to submit plans very far in advance. Part of the difficulty comes from inexperience, but the condition may result from being unaware of what is needed and how it should be presented. Some student teachers may be accustomed to presenting papers at the last minute at college and this may continue into student teaching.

It is important for a supervising teacher to examine plans before the student teacher actually uses them, especially in the earlier lessons. The following suggestions may help a teacher secure the plans in time to analyze them.

Provide a lesson plan form which is to be completed.
Indicate when the plans are to be submitted.
Prove to the student teacher that the plans are being carefully examined.
Make the requirements realistic.

Final decisions concerning some plans may have to be delayed until a previous lesson has been taught since most every plan needs some last-minute revision on the basis of the previous class activity. In spite of this the basic operating procedure of advance planning appears just as appropriate for student teachers as it does for experienced teachers. Plans ought to be ready far enough ahead so that effective organization for teaching is insured. Certain factors determine the format of advance planning. These points have to be assessed in determining the nature of advance preparation:

The necessity of advance planning for a particular class or unit
The progress of the student teacher
The amount of preparation which would be involved
The ability of the student to think in long-range terms
Time available for preparation
Availability of physical resources for planning.

Every effort should be made to see that plans are presented far enough ahead of time so that necessary revision can occur prior to teaching. This deadline should be governed by standards that are realistic. Asking student teachers, particularly new ones, to prepare plans a week in advance could pose a difficult task. Requirements for a great amount of unnecessary written work in planning can also prove to be an excessive task for some student teachers.

Case Study No. 33: LAST MINUTE PLANS

Your student teacher always has his plans but they come to you at the last minute. Because of this you only have time to give them cursory review before the class begins. You would like to see the plans earlier in order to suggest occasional revisions, but how do you go about telling him to submit the plans when you want them?

1. Specifically ask him to have the plans for you a certain number of days in advance.
2. Discuss the reasons why plans are submitted so late.
3. Deliberately discuss future lessons and explore the ideas verbally ahead of time.
4. _____

Comment:

The case study fails to indicate whether or not the supervising teacher and student teacher had discussed the matter of deadlines for plans. Many problems arise because one party makes an assumption which the other one is not aware of. The problem may relate to the student teacher's organizational style. Perhaps he completes all tasks at the last minute.

Questions:
1. What causes late planning?
2. Do student teachers present plans late in order to avoid analysis?
3. Will it work if a teacher states specific deadlines?

Case Study No. 34: MORE TIME NEEDED TO DEVELOP IDEAS

Sharon is a very creative person. She has some tremendous ideas for projects, but either she does not get started early enough to carry them through or she does not get started at all. The ideas are worthwhile, but you are puzzled about how to get her to think further in advance. What do you do?

1. Help her with the execution of some of her plans.

2. Suggest that she keep notes on her ideas and then try some of them when she has more time.
3. Ignore the ideas unless she actually can arrange to put them into practice.
4. _____

Comment:

Many people create more ideas than they can carry out. Sometimes they need encouragement in the development of these ideas; at other times they may need assistance in their implementation. Perhaps the supervising teacher may want to assist the student teacher while leading her to see how she could independently carry them to fruition by being better organized.

Questions:

1. Are creative people successful teachers?
2. Can it be detrimental if a teacher is too helpful?
3. Would too much emphasis on organization stifle the creativity of a person like this?

Case Study No. 35: THE STUDENT TEACHER IS UNPREPARED FOR AN ASSIGNED CLASS

Linda had volunteered to prepare materials for the children to use at the end of a unit, but she failed to produce them. When it came time to conclude the series she substituted prosaic activities giving no explanation to you.

As the two of you walk to the parking lot at the end of the day, Linda casually comments that she had not been prepared to teach the section which had been assigned to her because she went to a movie with her fiance the previous evening. You now understand why the materials were not ready.

What do you in this situation?

1. Resolve that you will always review plans at least one day in advance.
2. Determine to ask for all prepared materials at the beginning of each day.
3. Plan a conference with Linda and focus on the necessity of meeting responsibilities.

4. Dismiss the incident as an isolated situation which will probably not recur.
5. _____

Comment:

It appears that Option Number Two might be particularly worthy of consideration unless there is a valid cause for a schedule adjustment. This is possibly an isolated incident, but just in case the student teacher tends to be a bit immature, it might be well to have her accept the consequences of her decisions.

Questions:
1. Should student teachers be expected to be as responsible as their supervising teachers?
2. What should be done if a supervising teacher decides that the student's explanation was caused by the fact that she feels incapable of completing the project?

Case Study No. 36: FAILURE TO FOLLOW THE PLAN

Your student teacher is in his third week of student teaching and has responsibility for two classes. His plans are well structured and complete. The problem is that he tends to deviate from his plans and he frequently fails to do what he has proposed.

What do you do?
1. Ask for a copy of the plan while he is teaching.
2. Discuss the problem with him.
3. Give a quiz over the material which he should have covered and discuss the results with him.
4. Discuss the matter with his college supervisor.
5. _____

Comment:

In some cases it is beneficial to deviate from a plan. All teachers have done that. The question seems to be whether or not his teaching was effective and whether the content had value. If so, perhaps it would be worthwhile to call this fact to the attention of the student teacher and to encourage him to plan so that the substantive content is more likely to be pre-meditated.

Questions:
   1. What might cause a student teacher to deviate continually from his plan?
   2. How essential is it to closely follow a predetermined lesson plan?

SHARING PLANS AND RESOURCES WITH THE STUDENT TEACHER: **Opening the Confidential Files**

The person who fashions a new invention finds that a thorough knowledge of the field is necessary before one has the perception and imagination to attempt fresh ways of doing things. Since a lesson plan in many ways is an invention, it can be assumed that a student teacher's planning effectiveness will be in proportion to the knowledge that he has about alternatives. A student teacher who is cognizant of a variety of designs and opportunities should be able to plan more effectively than the one who has a more limited background.

Given the premise that creativity is based on knowledge, a supervising teacher will improve a student teacher's skill in planning by making available a variety of plans for different levels. It would be helpful to prepare a packet of model lesson plans for a student teacher. This collection could include objectives as well as projects and activities which help to achieve those goals. This knowledge can enrich the alternatives for a student teacher who is assuming responsibility for planning.

The sharing of plans must also include information about the facilities and resources which are available for developing an idea or process. A student teacher should have the opportunity to learn about and use some or all of the resources below.

Library resources
Audio-visual materials
   Films
   Filmstrips
   Recordings
   Tape recorders
   Video-tape-recorders
Available supplies and equipment
Community resources
   Public library

Service organizations
Business and industry
Available funds
Pupil talents
Publications
Resource materials within the teacher's classroom
   Publications
   Bulletin board material
   Equipment
   Supplies

Such materials and ideas may not have caught the attention of a student teacher. If a student teacher realizes the value of these resources and learns of their availability, he may tend to plan more creative activities rather than be dependent on the supervising teacher.

How does a teacher know how thorough and complete to be in guiding planning? Worksheet Number Nine in the Appendix presents a checklist which will serve as a frame of reference for a supervising teacher.

Case Study No. 37: THE STUDENT TEACHER ATTEMPTS TO IMITATE THE SUPERVISING TEACHER

Each teacher has to develop a style of teaching. A procedure that is ideal for one teacher may cause another to experience utter failure. You recognize this, but your student teacher has not yet been able to grasp this concept. Since you are an experienced teacher she is certain that whatever procedure you devise has to be superior to any of her techniques. Consequently, she observes you teach and then attempts to imitate your style. Instead of offering ideas for your approval, she asks for your ideas and then tries to follow them. Obviously she is experiencing little success and is becoming concerned about her ability to teach. What changes do you make to improve the situation?

1. Teach your class after the student teacher has taught, thus prohibiting imitation of the same lesson.
2. Indicate that she has followed your pattern; now you are going to follow her plans for a while in order to learn some different procedures from the ones which you have used.

3. Ask for her ideas and techniques in planning conferences.
4. Suggest that she observe other teachers for some ideas.
5. Explain why your procedures will not necessarily work for another teacher.
6. Express confidence in the student teacher's ability to create her own plans.
7. _____

Comment:
A student teacher should not emulate a supervising teacher. The description here seems to indicate that this student teacher is insecure and dependent. If the supervising teacher suddenly withdraws all support, the student teacher may experience a traumatic situation. Perhaps a gradual withdrawal would be less disturbing. The supervising teacher should consistently seek to support the student teacher's ideas in various ways.

Questions:
1. In this case should a teacher share any plans with a student teacher?
2. Do teachers unconsciously encourage student teachers to follow their procedures?
3. What 'steps can be initiated to encourage greater independence in planning?

Case Study No. 38: FAILURE TO LOOK AT THE PLANS

A methods professor at the university strongly urged her students to make use of every minute in the class. Cathy came to your school determined to meet those expectations convinced that it was her mission to teach and not to waste time. Since she seemed to have a lot of drive and due to a busy schedule, you failed to review the plans for her first lesson. It is a decision that proved to be unfortunate because Cathy was making greater demands on the class than you have been making and student discontent will quickly develop.

What do you do?
1. Find a way to assume control of the class as quickly as possible.

2. Watch carefully and be available in case of need.
3. Let the situation develop and resolve to confer very thoroughly with the student teacher about requirements.
4. _____

Comment:

The case study emphasizes the need for advance planning. The student teacher's objectives are undoubtedly worthy but she may not understand how they are incorporated into an ongoing program. The problem is to recognize any value in her ideas while looking for acceptable alternatives which will keep the class proceeding smoothly.

Questions:

1. How does a teacher reconcile differences in classroom practices with recommendations of a methods professor?
2. What questions would you ask Cathy about her goals and plans?

The class had ended and Brian returned to the teachers' room where Miss Bennett had been working.

"How was the lesson?"

"Better than yesterday," Brian was quick to report. "I had several examples this time and there were no lapses of time because there was not enough for them to do."

"How was the timing?"

"It seemed to be much better than before. I didn't stay with any one activity longer than fifteen minutes."

"I think that is best for this class," commented Miss Bennett.

Brian mentioned that Bill had asked him in class why they had to study all that 'stuff'.

Miss Bennett inquired, "What did you tell him?"

Brian relaxed, "I recalled that intensive examination you gave me yesterday in regard to objectives and explained why it was important and he seemed to accept it. And I thought you were putting me on when you were interrogating me in regard to purposes."

"You cannot be too well prepared to teach that group," noted Miss Bennett. "I have always felt that it is better to prepare thoroughly than it is to remediate because of insufficient planning."

Brian instantly responded, "I completely agree. I would have been in difficulty if I had not planned for this lesson well in advance."

Miss Bennett smiled as she closed her grade book. "You are making real progress, Brian. Continue to plan well and you will prevent difficulties from occurring."

Remember:

A student teacher needs to understand that planning facilitates good teaching.
A well-developed lesson plan may be a student teacher's best teaching aid.
Emphasis on results should prevail over emphasis on form.
It is helpful for the student teacher to be familiar with the supervising teacher's plans.
Good planning depends on an adequate concept of purpose and a knowledge of the learning rate of pupils.

USEFUL REFERENCES

ASSOCIATION FOR STUDENT TEACHING (Now Association of Teacher Educators), **Guiding Student Teaching Experiences,** Bulletin No. 1, 1968, pp. 12-14.

BENNIE, WILLIAM A., **Supervising Clinical Experiences in the Classroom,** Harper and Row, New York, 1972, pp. 95-98.

LANG, DUAINE C., QUICK, ALAN F., and JOHNSON, JAMES A., **A Partnership for the Supervision of Student Teachers,** The Great Lakes Publishing Company, Mt. Pleasant, MI., 1975, Chapter 5.

KNOP, CONSTANCE L., "Developing Student Teacher Skills in Lesson Planning and Self-Critiquing," **Foreign Language Annals,** 12:477-84, December, 1979.

TANRUTHER, EDGAR, **Clinical Experiences in Teaching for the Student Teacher or Intern,** Dodd, Mead and Co., New York, 1967, Chapter 4.

Chapter Seven

GUIDING TEACHING

Elaine Bennett strolled into the teachers' lounge and was confronted by a group of teachers who were unaccustomed to seeing her in the room in the middle of the morning.

"Not teaching today?" inquired Martha Wilson who normally has a break at this time.

"I am letting Mr. Sims teach the class this morning," Elaine replied.

The lounge lizards were quick to go to work on her.

"Sure must be nice," volunteered Toni Bridges, a second-year teacher who had not yet acquired the knack of being well organized. "I wish I could have someone to do my work for me and get extra pay for it."

"Best thing you ever did," roared Joe Hanley who possessed a notorious reputation for abandoning his student teachers. "Should have left him after the second day. They can't teach while you're in the room. They need to be left by themselves. I tell my student teachers that they can find me here if they need me. Otherwise I will know they are getting along all right. Gives 'em confidence to be left alone."

"Perhaps I am from the old school, but I think we should not turn our classes over to a neophyte." All eyes turned to Sylvia Rose, who had a reputation for having high standards. "I want to know what goes on in my classes, and the students these days will take advantage of a student teacher. Besides, you have to keep a close watch on some of these student teachers or they will be teaching a lot of nonsense to our children. A supervising teacher should be in the room all the time seeing that the student teacher is doing what is right."

Miss Bennett frowned, "I was following Brian's wishes and what I understood to be the guidelines of the university. He felt that he was ready to be left alone for a while. I think he needs to have this kind of responsibility occasionally."

"Sure he does," boomed Hanley.

"I don't think you can help a student teacher if you do not know what is going on in the class," countered Miss Rose.

Toni Bridges interjected, "All I know is I wish I had the opportunity to use one in my class. I sure need the help."

Miss Bennett quickly finished her coffee, excused herself, and was last seen heading for the library.

SUPERVISING INSTRUCTION: Teaching From the Back of the Room

The task of providing effective instructional supervision is one of the most complex tasks in working with student teachers. The supervising teacher's responsibilities must range from helping the student teacher achieve emotional independence in the classroom to analyzing and developing teaching strategies. The supervising teacher must allow freedom while still being responsible. This delicate balance encompasses many phases of teaching ranging from planning to pupil evaluation.

The question of independent teaching experience is a concern of both supervising teachers and student teachers. A supervising teacher who has responsibility for the class may be reluctant to be absent with a beginner in charge. The student teacher's dilemma may be that of wishing to have the teacher present for support in case it is needed; yet feeling more comfortable when the teacher is not in the room during periods of instruction.

Observing the Student Teacher

The necessity of observation is obvious. Analysis and evaluation cannot be effectively made unless the supervising teacher is aware of the actual situation. The experience of being observed can inaugurate the beginning of self-analysis and communication with other professionals. In spite of these admitted values the problem remains that the student teacher can feel uneasy with a supervisor present in the classroom. The challenge confronting the supervising teacher is that of creating an environment which permits the student teacher to feel comfortable while being observed. A logical beginning is to recognize the conditions which cause a student teacher to feel uncomfortable. The following situations are more likely to create uneasiness on the part of the student teacher who is being observed:

A lack of thorough planning
A perception of inadequacy in fulfilling the role of teacher
A feeling that the observation is an evaluation
Too much writing by the observer, especially when it consists of notes that are not shown later to the student teacher
Facial expressions which convey disagreement, confusion, or boredom
Interruptions by the observer
Infrequent observations
Lack of constructive analysis on a continuous basis

Specific suggestions for making observations less threatening can be inferred from the above list of causes. The procedures summarized below may be useful in helping the student teacher feel more comfortable with observers present:

Create an open door policy in the classroom
Invite the student teacher to observe your work
When in the room, do something besides sit and look at the student teacher
Use discretion in writing
Arrange to work with an individual or a small group of pupils while the student teacher is involved in teaching
Show positive reinforcement through smiles and other encouraging facial expressions
Observe frequently
Avoid interruptions in class
Make follow-up suggestions that emphasize the improvement of learning for the class instead of criticism of the student teacher's performance

Complete professional development depends upon the ability of a teacher to perform an act, study it, and plan a future course of action which benefits from the prior experience. Independent teaching is a necessary condition in this procedure in that it provides an actual encounter with the classroom environment. The supervising teacher's role is to help the student teacher reflect upon the act, provide input of new information and thoughts, and guide in the formulation of a more comprehensive plan of action. The predominant goal in this process is for the student teacher to have the ability to be competent in performing and analyzing the teaching act. In order to accomplish this aim a great amount of discretion will have to be used in providing the proper experience at the correct time -- a desirable portion of observed teaching and an adequate amount of independent practice.

The amount of actual observation time has to be carefully determined. Unfortunately two patterns can develop which work to the detriment of a student teacher. The first, and perhaps the most damaging one, is when a teacher chooses to allow a student teacher to be alone most of the time. This prevents the opportunity to observe difficulties or to reinforce good teaching behaviors. In essence this places a student teacher in a trial and error situation, a questionable practice in any profession.

The other pattern is one in which a teacher almost never leaves the room while a student is teaching. In this case the student teacher does not have a chance to establish a teacher-student relationship because the supervising teacher will be the dominant person. It may cause a student teacher to be uneasy and to feel that the supervising teacher wants to monitor every move. It simply smothers growth.

A student teacher needs to have the class by himself often enough to feel a personal responsibility for the class and to develop confidence. The supervising teacher must be in the room enough to observe the teaching style of the student teacher for analytical and evaluative purposes. The balance between complete classroom responsibility and observed supervision is most likely to be achieved when the supervising teacher is in the room approximately one-half of the time. Observations are more effective if neither student teacher nor pupils can detect the pattern, i.e., in one day, out the next; visit the first part of the class; leave the last, or some other unpredictable format. When the trend of supervisory observations cannot be detected, the supervising teacher will be able to observe the more typical climate.

The supervising teacher is normally needed in the room a greater percentage of the time during the first few weeks than during the last few weeks. It is good practice to occasionally leave the student teacher alone for the entire day, but this should be done only when the supervising teacher is convinced that the student teacher has matured to the point of being able to assume full responsibility for the class. The student teacher should know at all times where the supervising teacher can be found or where a responsible school official can be reached in case of need or emergency.

Case Study No. 39: DECIDING WHETHER TO OBSERVE THE STUDENT TEACHER'S FIRST COMPLETE LESSON

It is the first day that your student teacher is to present a complete lesson. She has done well when you worked together, but she has never been challenged by a long presentation. She is understandably tense and you want to support her as best you can. Unable to decide whether you should remain with the class or leave the room, you finally ask which alternative she prefers. She indicates that your being in the room will make her more nervous but that it would be good to have you available if something happened. Given these conflicting feelings what do you decide to do?

1. Remain in the room.
2. Remain in the room until you are convinced that her progress will be satisfactory and then leave.
3. Remain in the room but be preoccupied with some other activity.
4. Leave the room but let her know where you will be.
5. Leave the room the first part of the class and return later to determine how she is progressing.
6. Listen outside the classroom where neither the student teacher nor pupils know you are listening.
7. _____

Comment:

The student teacher is probably asking for help. The supervising teacher will have to offer that assistance in a supportive environment. Although many student teachers tend to be relieved when the supervising teacher leaves, most will probably admit that they are glad to have him available for assistance. The supervising teacher's task is to be perceived as that of a helping person rather than a critical observer.

Questions:

1. What causes a student teacher's indecisiveness about having a supervising teacher observing in the room?
2. Why are student teachers apprehensive of observations by their supervising teacher?
3. Do you know of some unfortunate incidents which have occurred with teachers who have made choices to remain in the room?
4. Have there been unfortunate consequences by leaving the room on the first full day of teaching?

Case Study No. 40: THE STUDENT TEACHER WANTS TO BE LEFT ALONE

Your student teacher has had the responsibility of teaching one group of pupils for three days. His performance has not been very satisfactory, but you have refrained from making any criticism in order to give him an opportunity to develop confidence. He asks you on the fourth day if he might teach the class alone because he is self-conscious with you in the room. He feels that he would be more effective if he were left alone. What action do you take?

1. Respect his wishes and leave while he is teaching.
2. Indicate that you feel he may not yet be ready to be left alone.
3. Discuss his progress by reviewing his current difficulties and then indicate some methods of improving.
4. _____

Comment:

The student teacher in this case is apparently becoming more uncomfortable with the supervisor present as an observer. Before the supervising teacher makes a decision on the request it might be well to determine why the student teacher wants to be left by himself. The supervising teacher may learn that the student teacher feels that he is being judged, but the discussion may also reveal that he needs some help in specific areas. The problem may be further compounded if the supervising teacher leaves the student teacher alone without any discussion of progress.

Questions:

1. Is there any condition when delayed analysis is beneficial?
2. What are some acceptable guidelines for performance for the first three days?
3. What messages could the teacher be unconsciously sending to the student teacher?

Case Study No. 41: A SUPERVISING TEACHER FAILS TO OBSERVE FOR SEVERAL DAYS

You are convinced that you have a competent student teacher. He has met every task to your satisfaction for several weeks. Since he has been doing well, you have taken the opportunity to catch up on some work and have not observed him for two weeks. Now you begin to wonder if you should visit the class more frequently. When you mention this to your student teacher, he seems mildly surprised and his response is that he feels that he does not need help. How do you respond?

1. Suggest that you might be able to help him initiate more sophisticated teaching techniques.
2. Indicate that you have left him alone because you have been busy.
3. Mention that you must write a final evaluation and that you want to have evidence of his more recent performances for that evaluation.
4. Stress that you are interested in learning some ideas from him.
5. State that it is always a good idea to have another person study a teacher's work regardless of his level of performance.
6. _____

Comment:

The unexplained absence apparently was interpreted by the student teacher to mean that he was performing unsatisfactorily. Since the supervising teacher has returned without any apparent explanation, the student teacher may feel threatened. There will have to be some explanation which will indicate that the return is designed to help make student teaching a better experience.

Questions:

1. What are some ways of reinforcing student teachers without being in the class?
2. What was the basic error which the supervising teacher committed?
3. What are some performance cues that cause a teacher to believe that a student teacher is doing well?

Interrupting The Student Teacher

The design of a student teaching program unavoidably creates a degree of anxiety. A teaching candidate is being scrutinized by an individual who has been recognized for teaching competence and his future may rest upon the judgment of this experienced teacher. The student teacher is in the process of facing problems with subject matter, classroom management, student behavior or teaching technique. Any criticism made by the supervising teacher may be disconcerting if it is made in the presence of a group of pupils.

Since the supervising teacher has to be concerned with the progress of the class as well as the growth of the student teacher, it is tempting to break into class with comments that are intended for the benefit of both. He may not understand the student teacher's feelings or comprehend the possible change in attitude the class might have toward the student teacher.

A supervising teacher is most likely to be tempted to interrupt in a class whenever:

A student teacher makes an error in subject matter.

The supervising teacher wishes to provide supplementary knowledge or an illustration.

The supervising teacher feels that a pupil should be corrected or disciplined.

The student teacher gets into difficulty and does not know how to overcome it.

Supervising teacher interventions are usually disconcerting experiences for a student teacher. Regardless of the teacher's good intentions, the student teacher may find it difficult to regain composure after a supervising teacher has interrupted. The supervising teacher's unilateral entry into a class discussion may correct an immediate difficulty but it can initiate a more serious problem. Such an intervention can produce a lack of confidence on the part of the student teacher and a deterioration of pupil respect. It can convey the idea that the student teacher is merely responding to directions. Interruptions should occur only when irreversible damage is being done to the class.

A good planning conference between the supervising teacher and student teacher should alert both parties to any potential problems and they can discuss methods of avoiding them if they do occur. Most other concerns can be discussed after class and then the student teacher can make the necessary adjustments in an ensuing session. A mistake in content, for example, can usually be explained by the student teacher the following day with no real problems as far as the pupils are concerned.

Case Study No. 42: THE STUDENT TEACHER NEEDS HELP DURING CLASS

The student teacher is teaching one of his more complicated lessons and you are observing from the side of the room. Although he has done a lot of study and preparation, he fails to develop many points in the presentation and hurries from topic to topic. His planned forty-minute lesson is completed in half that time. He has nothing else to say and you know that the study period will not keep students occupied the remainder of the time. He finishes his exercise and looks at you. What do you do?

1. Say nothing and let him experience the longer period of time with no planned activity.
2. Take over the class and provide additional explanation of material which has just been covered.
3. After the pupils have finished their study, start a discussion of some type which will consume the time remaining.
4. Say nothing but demand that the pupils follow the student teacher's instructions if confusion occurs.
5. _____

Comment:

There is no indication that the student teacher suspects difficulty. Any early move on the supervising teacher's part may be interpreted to be unnecessary. Perhaps an opportunity will occur for the student teacher to signal the supervising teacher. Otherwise, the implications from Option Number Three might appear to be the least threatening to the student teacher. Incidentally, this case would indicate that a planning conference would have been very beneficial.

Questions:
1. Does the teacher's room position determine whether he should interrupt?
2. Is it advisable to deliberately permit a student teacher to encounter difficulty?

Case Study No. 43: THE STUDENT TEACHER PRESENTS CONTRADICTORY INFORMATION

The content of some topics can be approached by more than one method. All can be adequate, but continuity is important if the pupils are not to be confused. The impact of this is made apparent to you one day during a demonstration when the student teacher suggests steps which are contrary to those you have already taught and which may cause the students to be confused. As the student teacher explains his system, several puzzled pupils look your way knowing that you had given them different instructions. What do you do?

1. Interrupt and explain that each method is satisfactory, but that they should follow your plan since it has already been inaugurated.
2. Remain silent and see what happens.
3. Discuss the problem after class and suggest a method of reconciling the differences in technique.
4. Permit the student teacher to continue with his approach.
5. _____

Comment:

A postscript to this section might say that there are justifiable interruptions. Any move on the part of the teacher must consider the welfare of the pupils. The teacher's dilemma is to inform the students while seeing that the student teacher maintains credibility with the class. If the teacher interrupts, a low-key approach may be best.

Questions:
1. How can the suggestions above be satisfactorily implemented?
2. What cues can be arranged so that a teacher can interrupt with the sanction of the student teacher?
3. Is this a case which would justify interruption?
4. Is it advisable to wait until the student teacher perceives the problem?

Case Study No. 44: THE STUDENT TEACHER WHO THINKS THAT COMPETITION IS THE KEY TO SUCCESS

Your student teacher is an advocate of pupil competition, but your pupils have been oriented more toward cooperation, competing only against themselves. As the student teacher assumes more responsibility for the class and advocates competition, pressure is increasing within the group and rivalries are appearing. The whole personality of the class seems to be changing and cooperation seems to be disappearing. You suspect that the quality of work is also regressing. The student teacher sees only the level of competition and is really enthused about it. What do you do?

1. Avoid any intervention until you can determine whether the competitive atmosphere will eventually produce positive results.
2. Speak to the student teacher and explain that competition sometimes has negative as well as positive effects.
3. Talk with the pupils privately (especially those most involved in rivalries) and try to explain what the student teacher is attempting to accomplish.
4. Compare test results and then evaluate whether competition is producing learning.
5. _____

Comment:

Although competition is widely advocated as a desirable process, one must examine the nature of the competition in this class and the impact that it will have upon all the pupils. Competition produces winners, but it also creates losers. If a student teacher is oriented toward competition, a supervising teacher must help the student teacher to analyze the total impact of such a procedure.

Questions:
1. What advantages are inherent in classroom competition?
2. Can the positive results sought by the student teacher possibly be achieved through cooperation, with the student teacher and

supervising teacher being models of such cooperation?

3. Is it fair to allow a student teacher to practice a technique which is inconsistent with a teacher's basic philosophy?

Case Study No. 45: IT IS DIFFICULT TO MAINTAIN CONTROL

Your student teacher seems to have difficulty demanding respect. Pupils just do not seem to listen to her while she is talking. In addition, she seems remiss in reminding pupils that they are not doing what is asked of them. You cannot perceive what she thinks of the situation but you want to help change it so that the learning climate seems better organized. What do you do?

1. Be patient, and wait for an invitation to intervene when difficulty is experienced.
2. Interrupt and make the necessary changes on the justification that first responsibility is for students' learning.
3. Discuss the matter in a conference at the first opportunity.
4. Video-tape the situation for the student teacher to observe.
5. Leave the room so that the student teacher will have to meet any challenges that occur.
6. _____

Comment:
There is the possibility that the student teacher may be aware of the situation but reluctant to discuss it because of the implication that she is unable to control the class. Direct interruption may not help but a frank discussion of the matter could be quite helpful. The video-tape might be used at a later time to identify particular problems.

Questions:
1. What is necessary to get respect from pupils?
2. How much of this condition can be attributed to the nature of the pupils?

Supervision By Cooperative Teaching

Cooperative teaching can be a valuable part of a student teaching experience throughout the entire period as well as during the initial days. It is a professional activity which has the potential for enriching teaching skills. Professional educators can learn from each other as they work together on a common task. Team teaching provides an opportunity for each teacher to use his better skills. The cooperative plan creates an opportunity for more creative activities as teachers working together pool their knowledge, ideas, and skills.

A cooperative arrangement has long been accepted as a procedure for induction into a profession or trade. The combination of mutual goals, shared responsibility, and contact with more experienced and more knowledgeable persons creates a climate for learning. The team situation provides an easier method for an individual to assume important responsibility. In the field of education, cooperation in more complex teaching situations is particularly desirable. Role definition is important in this type of arrangement. Each participant should understand his own sphere of operation and perceive that role as important to the accomplishment of the team task.

This team approach is especially recommended when the class can logically be taught in settings such as reading groups, physical education classes, and laboratory sessions. This method has the advantage of providing the opportunity for a supervising teacher to assist a student teacher who may be having problems without the pupils perceiving that difficulties exist.

Case Study No. 46: PUPILS TURN TO THE SUPERVISING TEACHER FOR ASSISTANCE

Your student teacher has assigned a project and you are in the room to see that it develops satisfactorily. Since the pupils are accustomed to working with you, they begin to come to you with their questions instead of asking the student teacher. There are now five students waiting to ask for your assistance while the student teacher has no one waiting for her help. What should you do?

1. Continue to help the pupils assuming that those waiting will go to the student teacher eventually.
2. Tell the pupils that Ms. _____ is the teacher

for this project and that she should be asked.
3. Quickly leave the room.
4. Announce to the class that both of you can give assistance if needed, but if one is busy the pupils should go to the other teacher.
5. _____

Comment:

Each option has an implication: The first one will likely find the supervising teacher doing most of the work since it is unlikely that students will turn to the student teacher for direction. Option Number Two takes the supervising teacher out of the picture in a situation which is supposed to be a team venture. Option Number Three has virtually the same effect, although the pupils might be more likely to turn to the student teacher without any further encouragement. Option Number Four clarifies for the students the working relationship between the supervising teacher and the student teacher.

Questions:
1. Is it more important to help the students or to give the student teacher more responsibility?
2. Is there any problem in continuing to work with the students?
3. What steps could be taken to prevent a problem such as this from arising?

Case Study No. 47: THE STUDENT TEACHER RESISTS WORKING WITH DIFFICULT GROUPS

In your highly-structured activity class, you have the pupils divided into ability groups and you have been rotating with the student teacher so that she can work with different levels. After a while she begins to seek means of avoiding working with the special needs section. She comments that she would like to work with the advanced group regularly because she does not ever intend to teach disabled students. She further states that she feels she is unable to accomplish anything with the slow learners. What is your response?

1. Let her work with the group she chooses.
2. Explain that she should be prepared for all levels

of teaching regardless of her present intentions.
3. Explain that this may be good preparation for working with brighter students.
4. Discuss techniques which will help her to be more effective with the problem group.
5. _____

Comment:

Most teachers enjoy classes which are made up of bright students; fewer want to work with those who have learning problems. It seems that it would ultimately be a disservice to the student teacher if she is removed from the situations which demand the greatest amount of teaching skill. However, the student teacher may need help, and this may be a good opportunity for the supervising teacher to suggest some ways which will make efforts with problem students more successful and rewarding.

Questions:

1. How can a supervising teacher better prepare a student teacher to work with slow learners?
2. How can a student be reinforced once she works with more difficult pupils?

ANALYZING TEACHING: **More Than Looking**

Teaching behavior can be described and modified. Behavioral characteristics can be subsumed into two major areas: (1) intellectual manipulation of subject matter, and (2) personal relationships between the teacher and students. A commission report by the Association for Student Teaching[1] on the study of teaching states:

"Student teaching in teacher education should offer opportunities for self-appraisal of the appropriateness of various styles of teaching for accomplishing specified objectives. Student teaching should be thought of as a time to study teaching as well as practice teaching. It is a time to put untried ideas to the test in a variety of real situations and to study the results.

---

[1]Commission on the Implications of Recent Research in Teaching. **The Study of Teaching**, Association for Student Teaching, (Now Association of Teacher Educators), 1967, preface.

"The study of teaching requires specialized skills. Prospective teachers can learn these skills, and supervisors can be trained to help preservice and inservice teachers in the study and practice of teaching as well as experiences which prepare supervisors in the study and practice of supervision."

A supervising teacher should help a student teacher to identify teaching skills and to incorporate them into a personal style of teaching. Many different descriptions exist, but the following criteria were developed in a research project concerned with factors related to success in student teaching.[2] This profile represents the positive teaching behaviors that were identified in that endeavor.

Understanding, friendly
> Friendly, understanding, tactful, good-natured
> Shows concern for a pupil's personal needs
> Tolerant of errors on the part of pupils
> Finds good things in pupils and calls attention to them
> Listens encouragingly to pupils viewpoints

Planned and organized
> Businesslike, systematic, consistent, thorough
> Presents evidence of thorough planning
> Objectives are clearly discernible
> Tells class what to expect during the period
> Has needed materials ready
> Keeps good records

Stimulating and imaginative
> Original, encourages pupil initiative
> Interesting presentation -- holds student interest
> Animated, enthusiastic
> Capitalizes on student interest

Possesses self-confidence
> Sees self as liked, worthy, and able to do a good job
> Speaks confidently; poised in relations with students
> Takes mistakes and criticisms in stride
> Accepts new tasks readily

Mastery of subject matter
> Recognizes important and significant concepts and generalizations
> Focuses class presentations on these basic concepts

[2]Donald M. Sharpe, **Isolating Relevant Variables in Student Teacher Assessment,** U.S. Office of Education, 1969, Contract No. OEC-3-7-061321-0342.

Relates to other fields or traces implications of the knowledge

Communicates well and empathetically

Shows acute sensitivity to the perceptions of pupils

Makes presentations at level of understanding

Draws examples from interests of age group being taught

Makes effective use of media

Has no distracting mannerisms

Speaks well

Classroom discourse characterized by reasoning and creative thinking

Helps students go beyond specific recall of facts into an understanding and application of problem solving

Seeks definition of problems in class and leads the pupils to consider solutions

Asks open-ended questions (frequently asks "why")

Encourages application of knowledge

Encourages students to see the relationships of facts to each other

Directs attention to the logical operations in teaching

Seeks definition of terms

Points out differences between what is observed and what is inferred from the observation

Demands examination of evidence

Leads students to state assumptions

Examines beliefs and opinions

The student teacher's experience can be improved if the skills are recognized and developed. The supervising teacher can stress the importance of the various skills by demonstrating them while teaching and by assisting the student teacher in improving his ability to effectively use them in teaching.

Reconstructing Teaching Activity

Observation of teaching can be of more value to the student teacher if the experience can be reconstructed, the effectiveness of the teaching acts discussed, and alternatives considered. An analysis form, the **Teacher Classroom Activity Profile** was developed in the previously-described project[3] as

<hr />

[3]Ibid.

one efficient way of recording major classroom activities in sequence. Classroom activity can be subsumed into seven categories and recorded on the form below.

MN-Management (Non-learning)
   Management of classroom when the teacher is not attempting to teach, e.g., reading announcements, taking roll, distributing materials, organizing equipment, idle time, disciplining pupils, waiting for bell to ring

ML-Management (Learning)
   Management of classroom so that learning may occur but the teacher is not involved except in a managerial role, e.g., showing a sound film, administering a written examination, supervising study time, student reports

Presentation
   The presentation of subject matter by the teacher in some organized fashion, e.g., lectures, demonstrations, illustrated talks, blackboard presentation, reading

Recitation/Drill
   The solicitation of student responses which call for terse memorized data, oral testing to determine if assignments have been read, review questions, drill, and practice time

Discussion/Random
   Random discussion involving student-teacher interaction but without analysis or synthesis. "Stream of consciousness" discussion without any apparent focus or purpose except to consume time until the period is over.

LT-Logical Thinking
   Discussion which involves analysis and synthesis. The teacher is deliberately encouraging or permitting thinking to occur. This category is more than reciting or repeating something which has been learned or memorized.

Thinking Process
   Deliberate, conscious attention on the part of the teacher to the intellectual process, e.g., point out to the students the factual and/or logical basis of their thinking, pointing out errors in reasoning, examining the reliability and validity of evidence, defining terms, checking assumptions, examining the scientific method, examining values, seeking reason for conflicting opinions, examining the method of inquiry

The observer records a continuous line moving among the seven activities in three-minute intervals. If there is just a momentary shift in categories, a vertical line going up or down to the proper category should be made without interruption of the general flow of the regular profile graphs. It has been found helpful to indicate the time at the top of the three-minute interval columns, starting in Column 1 with the minute the class starts and then recording the time at three-minute intervals after that in the numbered squares. Explanatory notes are keyed to the column number which indicates that sequence of three-minute intervals. Evaluative comments are recorded in the section designated as "Anecdotal Records." Worksheet Number 10 in the Appendix illustrates a completed form.

The Teacher Classroom Activity Profile:

Describes
>   the way a teacher spends time in the classroom
>   the type of classroom intellectual activity
>   the number of activities utilized

Gives clues to
>   whether objectives are being met
>   organizational patterns
>   possible teaching problems

Enables a teacher
>   to reconstruct his own experience for examination
>   to formulate conclusions toward his success in teaching

Written Communication in Analysis

Effective communication is a problem in nearly any situation. The student teaching environment can make it even more difficult. Since accurate exchanges of ideas are imperative to a good student teaching program, every possible procedure has to be practiced in order to increase understanding and information sharing. A lack of spoken or written conversation can create confusion and nurture a climate of misunderstanding. Written comments can help prevent a real gap in communication and comprehension. A principal purpose of written communication is to encourage student teachers and cooperating teachers to think about teaching. This interplay of ideas can become a dialogue which serves as a record of past performance and a file of suggestions which could be applicable in future teaching.

A supervising teacher and student teacher can exchange

views and information in writing when conversation is not possible. A teacher observing a student may want to communicate several ideas while watching. Since conversation is impossible at this point and since thoughts that are not recorded may be forgotten, writing becomes a valuable procedure. Written comments can be useful in developing clarity of thinking because both supervising teacher and student teacher have the opportunity to consider precisely what they want to say. Some universities require their student teachers to keep a journal for this purpose. This running commentary has the advantage of describing the continuous progress of the student teacher.

In summary, written communication can achieve the following functions:

Evaluates the progress of the student teacher
    Provides immediate reaction to the teaching situation
    Offers suggestions for improvements
    Indicates why a lesson was well taught
    Provides encouragement for the student teacher
Makes a permanent record of useful teaching ideas
    How to manage certain situations in teaching
    How to cope with problems which arise in working with pupils
    Ideas for such procedures as introducing a lesson and interjecting variety into a classroom routine
    Sources of instructional materials and aids
Determines contractual arrangements
    Defines responsibilities
    Clarifies verbal agreements
Encourages reflection
    Helps the student teacher to think about teaching
    Examines ideas and practices
Provides a record of professional information
    School procedures and regulations
    Professional information about students

Written comments enhance communication between a student teacher and supervising teacher. This is true because the volume of communication is increased and dialogue can occur when the two parties are unable to talk. Such communication is even more beneficial when one realizes that the comments are available in written form and may be retained for further reference.

A stenographer's notebook provides a durable, usable form

for written conversation and the middle line serves as a natural dividing line for the responses of the two participants. An example of a bit of written communication is illustrated in Worksheet Number Eleven in the appendix. Note that inquiries may be initiated by either party.

Case Study No. 48: THE STUDENT TEACHER IS CONFRONTED WITH A CHEATING INCIDENT

Debbie, your student [a new] teacher, has had the responsibility for one class for the past two weeks with no apparent problems. Today, however, she appeared to be very upset after class. As you confer with her, you learn that one of the students was caught cheating on a test and she had informed him that he would receive a grade of zero on the test. The student became angry and abusive. He then stormed out of class. As a supervising teacher, what should you do?

1. Reprimand the student and demand that he apologize to the student teacher.
2. Arrange for a three-way conference between yourself, the student teacher, and the pupil to discuss the problem.
3. Support the student teacher by telling her that you would have handled the situation in the same way.
4. Tell the pupil that he can take the test over sometime when the student teacher is working with another class.
5. _____

Comment:

A negative reaction from one pupil can cause a new student teacher to feel that she is being confronted by all the class members. A typical reaction may be for the new student teacher to have doubts about the advisability of her response. The question of support from the [another] supervising teacher becomes critical.

Questions:

1. Should the student teacher's actions be supported by the supervising teacher even though the action may be open to question?
2. Could a supervising teacher have prevented this confrontation from happening?

Case Study No. 49: THE STUDENT TEACHER WHO IS
RELUCTANT TO WRITE

As a supervising teacher you feel that systematic
written communication is essential, but your student
teacher hesitates to put anything down on paper. He
constantly forgets his journal and does not respond to
your written comments. Since you feel that such communication is necessary, what do you do?

1. Inform him that the journal is to be in the room at
   all times and that you expect him to make entries
   in it.
2. Continue writing, although he does not give any
   indication of having read your comments.
3. Discontinue writing in deference to his wishes.
4. Discuss the situation with the student teacher
   and try to determine why he feels that such communication is not important.
5. _____

Comment:
Many student teachers resist written communication. A perceptive supervisor will also want
to determine whether this condition applies to oral
communication as well. It would also be well to
determine whether the student teacher understands the purpose of written communication.
This could be the essence of the problem.

Questions:
1. What kinds of written comments might
   encourage a student teacher to want to participate in written exchange?
2. What are some responses to negative reaction about the value of writing in a journal?

SUPERVISING PARTICIPATION IN PUPIL EVALUATION: **The
Curve Becomes a Question Mark**

One of the most exciting activities for the student teacher is
participation in the evaluation of pupil achievement. The student teacher who is allowed to share in this process should
feel that he has earned his teacher's confidence. A student
teacher's self-confidence can be quickly shattered, though,
when the complications of evaluating pupils begin to emerge.

The first test results can be more effective in criticizing a student teacher than all the exhortations of a supervisor. If the material was covered too rapidly or too abstractly, low test results will transmit the message. If the grades are too high, it is quite apparent that the test was too easy or that pupils were not being challenged. A student teacher may discover that the terminology or phrasing of a test was so obscure that the results cannot be considered valid.

The evaluation procedure provides the opportunity for a student teacher to gain a concept of pupil ability. The boy who had all the answers in class may have produced a rather unimpressive test response, and the girl whose name cannot be recalled may have the highest score in the group. Other visible cues of writing and expression may present an understanding of pupils which had evaded the student teacher so far.

The beginning student teacher is apt to possess a very limited concept of evaluation. A test may be considered to be the objective for teaching, and quizzes may be presented as devices which coerce students into completing assignments. Comments such as, "Read the chapter because we may have a test on it tomorrow," may accompany an assignment. A pupil may be referred to as an "A" or "D" student as if that designation presents a profile of a child. This is particularly true when it can be reinforced by quoting an IQ or achievement test score. Even more significant may be the fact that a student teacher may tend to view evaluation as an end instead of a process for instructional analysis. Evaluation may be determined by some poorly worded specific-recall questions instead of a more sophisticated examination.

The origin of this superficial concept of evaluation may have arisen from a lack of experience or from poor example. The student teacher will undoubtedly have a great amount of insight to gain and possible attitudes to alter in regard to evaluation. The supervising teacher can take nothing for granted here.

The joint approach to evaluation is usually preferable because it enables the supervisor to be in a position to help the student teacher develop a more adequate concept of appraisal. The objectives of this shared approach should lead to a student teacher's formulation of a comprehensive outlook in regard to evaluation. Consider the following as desirable goals to be achieved by the joint approach:

It should help the student teacher understand the role of pupil evaluation.

A tool for growth instead of an instrument for judgment
Pupil evaluation reports serve as teaching guides
It should help the student teacher understand the total process of evaluation.
Techniques of evaluation
Different types of examinations and quizzes
Methods in determining letter grades
It should help the student teacher understand what a student is capable of achieving.
It should ensure that the student teacher understands the criteria which can be considered in determining a grade.

After the student teacher gains some understanding of the evaluation process, this knowledge should be applied through participation in the determination of grades. The supervising teacher will want to review and approve the assigned grades before they are announced to the pupils. The student teacher can gain a lot of confidence if his evaluation roughly corresponds to that of the supervising teacher.

Case Study No. 50: THE GRADE IS NOT THE SAME

John has been assuming full teaching responsibility. Since he has been doing well you have decided to let him make out the six-week grades. When you check his report you find that he has given three B's, fifteen C's, and eight D's and two F's. Since the class has traditionally scored better than this, you question him about the lower grades. His explanation was that no student met his standards for an A. You disagree with this but feel frustrated because he has already told the students what their grades will be.

What do you do?
1. Tell the students that John made a mistake, consult with him, and raise the grades that should be changed.
2. Support the student teacher since this is only one part of the semester evaluation program.
3. Discuss the difference with the student teacher and jointly tell the class what has happened.
4. _____

Comment:
It seems as if the matter of standards must be discussed. Once agreement is reached, the

welfare of the pupils must be considered. The case appears more simple when one observes that the grades were reported orally. The case has a clear message for supervisors: discuss grades with the student teacher before they are announced to the class.

Questions:

1. What criteria should be used to determine the correct standards?
2. What are some possible agreements that a supervising teacher and student teacher can accept?
3. Should pupils pay the price if the student teachers standards are unrealistic?
4. How can the pupils be fairly treated without discrediting the student teacher?

Brian had been teaching about fifteen minutes when Miss Bennett returned to the room. As he continued, she cast a few knowing glances when he successfully made a difficult explanation. After a while she reached for the journal and entered a few comments.

When class was finished they discussed the development of the lesson. Miss Bennett began by inquiring about the introduction and then asked for Brian's reaction to the lesson. After his comments, she added, "I think that you showed considerable improvement in your development of thinking today. The questions caused the pupils to relate the material we have been working with for the last week. I think they will be more sophisticated in their future work because of this series of lessons."

Brian agreed and then glanced at the journal. Miss Bennett caught the cue and handed the book to him. "I recorded a thought or two about your teaching style in general as you had requested. A little attention to the details which I have mentioned can help you with a few of your concerns. I also wrote down some ideas for teaching the next unit which you might like to consider in your preparation."

While Brian was reading the comments, Miss Bennett continued organizing some materials which Brian had planned to use with the next group. During this time Joe Hanley walked by, looked in the room and a puzzled look formed on his face. He shrugged his shoulders and sauntered on toward the teachers' lounge.

Remember:

A student teacher is likely to imitate many of a supervising teacher's methods and techniques.

It is necessary for the supervisor to observe a student teacher but it is equally important to provide times when he can be alone with the class.

Student teachers tend to become concerned when they are interrupted by their supervising teachers.

Written communication is a valuable supplement to oral dialogue.
Student teachers must participate in evaluation as well as instruction.

USEFUL REFERENCES

ANDERSON, ROGER; LARSON, CHARLES; and SCHMALZRIED, DONALD, **Supervision by Objectives: A Model for Supervision of Clinical Students,** Professional Improvement Series for Supervising Teachers, Northern Illinois University, DeKalb, IL, 1979.

ARLIN, MARSHALL, "Teacher Transitions Can Disrupt Time Flow in Classrooms," **American Educational Research Journal** 16:42-56, Winter, 1979.

ARMSTRONG, DAVID G., "Equipping Student Teachers to Deal with Classroom Control Problems," **The High School Journal** 60:1-9, October, 1976.

CLOTHIER, GRANT, and KINGSLEY, ELIZABETH, **Enriching Student Teaching Relationships** (Supervising Teacher Education), Midwest Educational Training and Research Organization, Shawnee Mission, KS, 1973.

COPELAND, WILLIS D., and BOYAN, NORMAN, "Training in Instructional Supervision: Improving the Influence of the Cooperating Teacher," **Developing Supervisory Practice,** in ATE Bulletin No. 41, 1900 Association Drive, Reston, VA 22091.

DUVALL, CHARLES R., and KREPEL, WAYNE, J., "The Use of Videotape Recordings in the Analysis of Student Teaching Performance," **The Teacher Educator,** 7:1, pp. 12-16, Autumn, 1971.

GROSSHANS, ORIE R., "A Student Teacher Checklist: Professional Preparation," **Health Education** 9, 30-31, November, December, 1978.

MOORE, BARBARA A., "Improving Student Teacher-Cooperating Teacher Communication," **Agricultural Education** 51:92-3, October, 1978.

MOTT, DENNIS L., "Student Teaching by Objectives," **Journal of Business Education** 53:116-18, December, 1977.

SCHAIBLE, ANNE, and McCRACKEN, J. DAVID, "Dealing with Disruptive Behavior," **Agricultural Education** 52:39, August, 1979.

SHARPE, DONALD M., **Isolating Relevant Variables in Student Teacher Assessment,** U.S. Office of Education, 1969, Contract No. OEC-3-7-061321-0342.

SPANJER, R. ALLAN, **Teacher Preparation: Supervision and Performance,** Association of Teacher Educators, 1972.

TEMPLIN, THOMAS J., "Occupational Socialization and the Physical Education Student Teacher," **Research Quarterly** 50:482-93, October, 1979.

WALTER, JAMES E., "Classroom Control and Student Teachers," **School and Community** 61:13, April, 1975.

Chapter Eight

THE SUPERVISORY CONFERENCE

The university student teaching handbook suggested that a student teacher and supervisor conduct an extensive analysis of professional progress after a few weeks of student teaching. In accordance with this, Brian and Miss Bennett were discussing the details suggested in the handbook to see that all requirements were being met. Brian turned the page and said, "Look at this!" He began to read aloud.

"Conferences are as essential to the student teaching experience as teaching if maximum professional growth is to occur. This dialogue is a necessary procedure in providing complete analysis of the complex nature of teaching. A conference can help the student teacher solve immediate and long-range problems through the verbal input of the supervising teacher. Such conferences should be regular experiences for the teaching candidate."

Miss Bennett seemed mildly concerned. "Since you have been doing well, it has not seemed necessary to spend so much time in formal conferences. Do you think we should spend more time with such activity?" . . .

THE CONFERENCE: A Professional Mirror

A supervisory conference is verbal interaction which focuses on the professional growth of a student teacher. It is in contrast to the conversation that occurs between a teacher and a student teacher in that a conference stresses analysis, evaluation, information and ideas. Conversation, on the other hand, is more informal and is designed for the establishment of rapport, communication of personal thoughts, and relaxation. Informal talk is beneficial but a conference is essential in the development of a student teacher.

In a sense a conference is a professional mirror where a supervisor reflects a student teacher's performance by providing accurate feedback. A conference should help the student teacher perceive teaching more clearly and provide direction for action. It is a method of providing feedback concerning progress so that a student teacher knows and understands how the supervisor feels.

Roles and Responsibilities of Participants

A conference is most effective when participants understand the contributions which each one has to make in this dialogue. A supervising teacher must be responsible for seeing that a student teacher understands this concept. The supervising teacher structures the conference environment by determining the content, setting, procedure, and by establishing rapport.

The student teacher should also be a contributor to successful conferences. He has to arrange to be available for conferences at a convenient time and to make preparation by listing questions or topics which should be discussed. A student teacher should be an active participant and attentive listener. He should plan to express feelings, discuss ideas, ask questions, and take action which would indicate that the interaction has produced growth.

Case Study No. 51: THE SUPERVISING TEACHER HAS DIFFICULTY IN COMMUNICATING IDEAS

After a few conferences you have the feeling that your student does not understand what you are telling her. She looks puzzled when you talk and shows little response to suggestions. You begin to wonder if you are talking in generalizations and failing to deal specifically with relevant topics. What do you do?

1. Discuss this feeling with the student teacher.
2. Seek alternative methods of communication.
3. Talk the matter over with the college supervisor.
4. Modify your conference style in order to see if some other approach is more effective.
5. Put a conference on audio-tape or video-tape and look for clues.
6. _____

Comment:

The supervising teacher will need to determine why the student teacher is not responding. If it is due to a communication problem, it can probably be solved. If the student teacher is failing to act because of feelings of inadequacy, then the situation will be more complex.

Questions:

1. What kind of reasonable action should be expected of a student teacher after a conference?

2. Is the supervisor or the student teacher responsible for improving the situation?

THE CONFERENCE SCHEDULE: **Ready When You Are**

The effectiveness of a conference is in direct proportion to its timing. A good conference design will include both formal and informal conferences. The number, length, type, time, and location of each will depend upon the needs of the participants.[1]

Informal conferences are held as needed. The brief, informal conference keeps the lines of communication open at all times and allows for immediate feedback and idea sharing. The practice of meeting daily on an informal basis is conducive to the development of cooperative working relationships. If the supervising teacher and student teacher are accustomed to continuous interaction, they will find themselves discussing relevant topics in a casual environment which is less threatening than a strict supervisor-student atmosphere.

Spontaneous conferences shuld be supplemented by formal conferences. These sessions should be scheduled for a specific time and include a planned agenda of topics which relate to the development of teaching competency. A typical agenda might include a discussion of strengths and weaknesses, planning, information about the school and students, and specific analysis of teaching behaviors. These should be scheduled in a place and at a time when interruptions would normally not occur.

Initial Conferences

Initial conferences provide opportunities for a student teacher and supervising teacher to get acquainted. The teaching candidate may feel uneasy in this new situation, and the supervising teacher can also have some feeling of uncertainty. The initial conference can establish a mutual bond and working relationship between the two persons. The supervising teacher must be cognizant of the fact that the student teacher may need assistance in making the transition from university student to classroom teacher. If such assistance is to be effec-

[1]Louise Dieterle, **Holding Conferences With Student Teachers,** Office of Clinical Experiences, Illinois State University, 1976, p. 1.

tive, it will be necessary for the supervising teacher to learn as much as possible about the student teacher.

The initial conference or conferences should include:

Orientation to the school including its philosophy and rules
Discussion of procedural matters
Explanation of the role the student teacher is to perform
Suggestions for activities for the student teacher during the
  first few days
Information about supplies and equipment
Information about the classes
Information about the school and community
Explanation of the supervising teacher's philosophy and pro-
  cedures
Questions about the student teacher's background, interests,
  and experiences
Discussion of personal considerations which could affect stu-
  dent teaching

Developmental Conferences

Developmental conferences are those ongoing contacts that occur after completion of the initial concerns and encompass the major part of the program. They include both informal and formal contacts.

The conference agenda will usually be determined by the supervising teacher although the student teacher should feel free to provide input as needs dictate. The content of the conferences will depend upon the student teacher's rate of development and upon the amount of experience that has accrued. It can safely be assumed that a student teacher will be receptive to a performance analysis when a lesson has been completed. He may be more than ready for a discussion of teaching technique or classroom management after a frustrating experience with a class or a pupil. The needs of the moment frequently serve as the agenda for productive conferences.

Developmental conferences should eventually cover a wide range of topics which are essential to success. A complete and thorough conference will involve the following topics at least once:

Analysis of teaching skills
  Development of subject matter
  Affective teaching qualities
  Teaching techniques
Evaluation of the student teacher's progress
  Discussion of whether learning is occurring
  Identification of skills which the student teacher
    possesses
  Review of the student teacher's concept of teaching
  Discussion of deficiencies and how to overcome them
  Periodic review of the final evaluation form
Information about students
  Cumulative record information
  Personal observations and insights
  Student behavior as related to psychological concepts
Sharing professional ideas and knowledge
  Philosophy of grading and evaluation
  Ideas on discipline and classroom management
  Techniques for efficient organization
  Coping with the unexpected
  Professional organizations
Discussion of plans
  Pre-teaching analysis
  Post-teaching appraisal
  Ideas for long-range planning
  Activities and techniques which can be incorporated into
    planning
Personal adjustment
  Personal problems and their effect on the school setting
  Relationships with students
  Relationships with other faculty members
  Values as they relate to teaching
Additional experiences which might be beneficial
  Observations
  Activity levels
  Teaching procedures

Summary Conferences

Summary conferences provide opportunities to review the experience, to evaluate the present condition, and to project future directions. Although conferences of this nature will be conducted at the termination of the experience, it seems logical that a series of conferences are in order during the last few days.

During the final conference experiences the topics for discussion should include:

Review of the university's final evaluation form
Review of goals for student teaching and whether they were
  met
Discussion of growth
Discussion of areas needing improvement
Student teacher's reflection about teaching

Case Study No. 52: MORE CONFUSION THAN RESULTS

At the initial conversation you explained a number of details ranging from procedures for checking attendance through a description of the social structure of the school community. Your student teacher seemed interested and even made notes during the conference. The concern came near the end of the session when she appeared to be more confused than informed and asked several questions about information which you just covered. What do you do?

1. Continue the conference and answer the questions.
2. Indicate that you may have given too much information and suggest a later follow-up conference.
3. Summarize your major points in written form and give them to her for study.
4. Ask her to summarize what she has been told.
5. _____

Comment:

Two factors seem to be operating in this instance. First it can be hypothesized that the teacher is presenting too much information at one time. The second would indicate that the student teacher is too unorganized and perhaps too inexperienced to comprehend much of the content. A carefully planned and well organized system of conferences would be more helpful.

Questions:

1. What would you consider to be priority information for an initial conference?
2. How can a teacher help a student teacher assimilate information?

Case Study No. 53: NO CONCEPT OF PROGRESS

You had planned carefully for the mid-term conference and presented a summary of strengths and conditions that needed improvement. You finished with an optimistic statement indicating that Sharon should be a strong teaching candidate by the end of the experience. You then asked her for a self-appraisal. Her comments showed that she possessed a superficial concept of what was actually involved in teaching. In a sense she felt that she was half way through another college requirement; no more, no less. This reaction concerns you. What response do you make?

1. Question her further to determine how well she understands the goals of teaching.
2. Explain why student teaching is significantly different from traditional college course work.
3. Work on a sequence which will insure that the student teacher is aware of her teaching potential by the end of the experience.
4. _____

Comment:

It may be difficult for a student teacher to see the difference between course work and student teaching. It is further complicated because self-analysis is a critical factor. A teacher needs to be aware that this condition may exist and to help the student teacher assume a different perspective.

Questions:

1. How can a student gain an appreciation of the impact of student teaching?
2. What can a teacher do to help a student teacher improve skills in self-analysis?

Case Study No. 54: THE STUDENT TEACHER AVOIDS SCHEDULED CONFERENCES

One of your major difficulties has been the problem of getting your student teacher to participate in conferences. He seems to find other things to do during conference time or indicates that he does not have any questions. When you do manage to sit down together, he gives perfunctory answers to your questions and then attempts to steer you into conversations about topics which are not directly related to his student teaching. Since you are convinced that conferences are necessary, what do you do?

1. Arrange a specific time each day for conferences and have an agenda.
2. Attempt to structure these sessions so that the student teacher feels more comfortable.
3. State the reasons for the conferences so that he will understand the rationale for these sessions.
4. Abandon any further attempts until he makes some gesture indicating interest.
5. _____

Comment:

It would appear that the student teacher either sees little need for conferences or is attempting to avoid confrontation with some of his problems or weaknesses. It is tempting to follow choice Number Four but that would simply postpone getting to the core of the problem. It may be well to examine what has occurred previously and then to structure a conference which has substance to it. It would seem that an agreement should be made about conference times and that agendas should be prepared.

Questions:

1. Why would a student teacher avoid conferences?
2. What are some positive ways for making this experience more acceptable for the student teacher?
3. What do teachers often do to indicate that they also wish to avoid conferences?

EFFECTIVE CONFERENCE COMMUNICATION: **More Than Talk**

Conference structure is merely a form which leads to effective communication. One study has shown that the most common critical incident perceived by student teachers was a lack of communication between the cooperating teacher and the student teacher. The authors in the study state that a supervisor must be skilled in dealing with interpersonal relationships. One of the necessary skills seems to be that of facilitating and encouraging communication between the cooperating teacher and the student teacher.[2] The conference is more likely dominated by affective behaviors than by cognitive concerns.

The conference provides a challenge in human relations. An attitude of mutual trust and respect has to prevail. If either party is reluctant to confer, a strained relationship usually results. If a student teacher fears the situation for one reason or another, his response may be negative. A poor choice of words or an ill-chosen expression can create unnecessary tension. The Association for Student Teaching (now the Association of Teacher Educators) makes several suggestions in its bulletin relating to supervisory conferences:[3]

The supervising teacher must learn to listen.
> Do not get so busy formulating responses that you fail to listen to what is being said.

Try to meet the needs expressed by the student teacher.
> Information
> Reassurance
> Evaluative comments

Understand how the student teacher feels in the situation.
> Project empathy

Maintain objectivity during conferences.
> Emphasis should be placed on what actually was said and done rather than on opinions of what occurred.

Self analysis should be encouraged through the conference because it is one of the most effective ways to produce change. This can allow the supervisor to guide a student teacher instead of lecturing to him.

The key to encouraging self appraisal is to encourage it through a series of relevant questions. Paul Myers[4] has developed a model which is designed to assist student teachers in evaluating and analyzing their teacher selfhood. Each consideration is in the form of a question so that the supervising teacher will resist the temptation to provide answers. The model with accompanying questions is submit-

[2]Carey Southall and Dorothy F. King, "Critical Incidents in Student Teaching," **The Teacher Educator**, Fall, 1979, pp. 34-36.

[3]Association for Student Teaching, **Supervisory Conference as Individualized Teaching**, Bulletin No. 28, 1969, pp. 25-29.

[4]Paul E. Myers, "The Real Crux of Supervision," **Contemporary Education**, XLIV:3, January, 1973, pp. 140-141.

ted as a guide for consideration for the encouragement of reflection:

A. Questions Relating to Background Preparation
   1. What are your present conclusions regarding your preparation to teach? Consider the following:
      a) How well prepared were you in your subject matter area?
      b) Were you psychologically prepared to deal with today's youth?
      c) Have you had some up-to-date experiences with young people?
      d) Did you have some knowledge of the contemporary public schools?
B. Questions Relating to Aptitudes for Teaching
   1. Are you beginning to view yourself as a teacher rather than as a student?
   2. Do you feel you have some unique characteristics that make you interesting to students? What are they?
   3. Have you honestly examined your attitude toward young people in general and toward your pupils in particular?
   4. Do you like and enjoy the overall climate of the public school?
   5. What is the present status of your confidence? Do your periods of depression and discouragement last more than a day or so?
   6. What do you think students think of you?
   7. Do you feel you have potential you have not yet realized?
   8. Are you able to derive honest satisfaction from your excursion into teaching?
   9. How do you respond to advice and criticism?
   10. How willing are you to do some honest thinking about teaching and your potential within the profession?
C. Questions Relating to Attitudes Toward Teaching
   1. How do you view the profession of teaching and those who teach?
   2. What do you see in the future for the profession?
   3. Is your attitude generally one of optimism and enthusiasm?
   4. Are you thoroughly convinced of the significance of teaching of the public school in our present culture?

5. Have you been completely honest with yourself as you have answered these questions?

The supervising teacher will occasionally have to make suggestions and take actions which will test communication skills. Although much is demanded of the supervising teacher in the conference, the reward will come when the student teacher shows growth and understanding.

The supervising teacher should be aware that non-verbal factors in communication will be more believable than verbal utterances. The following moves will influence the receiver's attitudes about conversation:

Facial expressions
> Eye contact (Involves looking but not staring at the person who is talking)
> Head nods (Affirmative nods, used occasionally, indicate that one is listening)
> Facial looks (smiles, frowns, quizzical looks, etc.)

Body positions
> Sitting positions
> Posture

Vocal responses
> Voice tones
> Inflections
> Volume
> Phrasing

All conference content is irrelevant unless a favorable emotional climate exists. One of the better ways of creating that climate is to be a good listener and resist the temptation to lecture or to judge. Sixty-five percent of the talk in a supervisory conference is initiated by the supervising teacher. This may be as it should be but a teacher should also seek as much verbal balance as possible.

The conference setting is also a part of successful communication. Many conferences will be brief and spontaneous; others will be planned and more deliberate. In either event, the exchange should be private and conducive to an attitude of reflection.

An effective conference has interaction which is problem centered rather than personality centered. Each participant should be able to recommend topics for discussion and to consider suggestions for problems. Each should feel comfortable and secure enough to make the conference situation a real individualized teaching encounter.

Case Study No. 55: THE AGREEABLE, BUT UN-CHANGING STUDENT TEACHER

Your student teacher is as cooperative in his conversation as one would want. The problem is that he seldom follows through on any of the points which have been agreed upon. In spite of your efforts, he just continues to agree with you and then proceeds as if you had never talked. What do you do in this situation?

1. If it involves agreement on concrete items such as the submission of plans, refuse to let him proceed with activity until he meets the conditions agreed upon.
2. Instead of asking him to agree, force him to make statements or comments and then concur with him.
3. Be more demanding In following through when conditions are not met.
4. Write agreements down so there is a concrete record.
5. _____

Comment:

Sometimes an individual will agree to anything regardless of how he feels. It may be fair to assume that this is the case here. Change may be difficult to bring about. Perhaps a look at each alternative may help to see the implications: 1) This will confront him with the fact that you mean what you say. Will it cause him to ask any additional questions if he does not understand? 2) Statements may be vague and may be an attempt to guess what you want. 3) You may get more agreement but little change. 4) This may clarify information in case of misunderstanding.

Questions:

1. How can a supervising teacher determine whether ineffective communication is causing the problem?
2. What non-verbal moves on the part of the supervising teacher may be beneficial?

Case Study No. 56: THE DEFENSIVE STUDENT TEACHER

The conference period had been strained between you and the student teacher from the very beginning when he was uncomfortable with your early endeavors to explore his background and interests. Now that he has started teaching, your attempts at analyzing the lesson seem to bring negative reactions. He expresses satisfaction with his work and implies that nothing needs to be discussed. When suggestions for improvement are made, he disagrees with you and says that he is teaching the way he was instructed by university professors. Since little progress is being made, what course of action do you take?

1. Eliminate or reduce the number of conferences.
2. Try to revise your procedure and become more student centered.
3. Inform him that he should make an honest effort to change before it is too late.
4. Concentrate only on topics where some agreement or consensus can be reached.
5. Attempt to indicate that you understand his feelings.
6. _____

Comment:
The problem could have many causes ranging from student insecurity to the conference style of the supervising teacher. If the student teacher can be convinced that the supervising teacher has some empathy, communication may be possible. A review of Gazda's **Human Relations Development** which is cited at the end of this chapter may be beneficial.

Questions:
1. What are some possible causes of the student teacher's behavior?
2. What guidelines may be established for adjusting to a student teacher who presents an attitude similar to the one in this case study?

The class terminated and Brian had a period of time to confer with Miss Bennett. He was anxious to know what she thought of his technique, especially since he planned to use the same procedure in subsequent lessons.

Brian began, "They sat down at their tables and showed more interest than usual and seemed to handle the discussion questions with more insight than I had expected."

Miss Bennett agreed, "I felt that they were able to comprehend the reasons behind the questions and they had some supportive facts. What did you think of your introduction?"

Brian thought, and slowly responded, "I guess it was not too good."

Miss Bennett responded, "But it was not all bad. Why did you think it was not so good?"

Brian quickly replied, "They did not pay close attention and it could have been difficult for them to see how it related to the later questions."

She inquired, "How could it have been made better?"

Brian considered the question and then speculated that an actual recording of the event or some dramatic statement might have commanded more thinking.

Miss Bennett accepted his evaluation and further stated, "You might use the board to list important ideas, too. One other point, did you notice that you directed most of the questions to six students - Jo, Jan, Greg, Tom, Rex, and Carla?"

"Did I?" exclaimed a surprised Brian. "Now that I think of it, I believe that is right. I will have to go beyond those who are wanting to talk all the time. I will try to draw Kirsten and Abbie into the discussion tomorrow."

Miss Bennett smiled and then gave an endorsement to Brian's technique which he had tried for the first time. The conference drifted into conversation, and they left feeling that the session had been productive.

Remember:

A conference should involve the free flow of ideas which will foster an objective analysis of the student's teaching ability.

A conference should be problem-centered instead of person-centered.

A conference should be constructive with the student teacher feeling that it has helped in some way.

A conference should be private.

A good conference should lead to concrete plans of action which are useful in guiding future activities.

The conference is the period of time when the supervisor interacts most effectively with the student teacher.

Frequent conferences are less threatening than infrequent conferences.

Conferences should be concerned with matters considered to be important by their participants.

Conferences should lead to satisfaction on the part of the participants.

The teacher who learns to listen in conferences will be better able to help the student teacher analyze his own teaching behavior.

USEFUL REFERENCES

AICHELE, DOUGLAS B., and CASTLE, KATHRYN, **Student Teaching: A Cooperative Experience,** Parts V and VIII, Oklahoma State University, 1979, ERIC ED 175 461.

BAER, G. THOMAS, **The Cooperating Teacher - Some Hints for a Successful Experience,** Illinois State University, ERIC ED 117 086.

BENNIE, WILLIAM A., **Supervising Clinical Experiences in the Classroom,** Harper and Row, New York, 1972, pp. 91-95.

BYERS, CHARLES and BINKLEY, HAROLD, "The Role of Conferences in Developing a Competent Student Teacher," **Agricultural Education Magazine** 48:116-17, Nov. '75.

ELLENBURG, F. C., "Discussion Topics for Evaluation Time," **Instructor** 86:83, October, 1976.

GAZDA, GEORGE, **Human Relations Development,** Allyn and Bacon, New York, 1973.

HEITZMANN, WILLIAM RAY, "The Classroom Teacher and the Student Teacher," NEA, Washington, D.C., 1977, ERIC ED 146 152.

HEMP, PAUL E., "Conducting an Effective Critique Conference," **Agricultural Education Magazine** 51:30, 33, August, 1978.

LANG, DUAINE C., QUICK, ALAN F., and JOHNSON, JAMES A., **A Partnership for the Supervision of Student Teachers,** The Great Lakes Publishing Company, Mount Pleasant, MI., 1975, Chapter 7.

KENNEDY, EDWARD, "Postobservation Conference," **Journal of Physical Education and Recreation** 49:73, May, 1978.

MICHALAK, DANIEL, "Kinesics: A Useful Tool in Teacher-Student Communication," **The Teacher Educator,** 10:2, pp. 37-40, Winter, 1974-75.

_____, **Supervising Conferences in Field Experiences,** Missouri ATE occasional Paper No. 4, June, 1977.

MYERS, PAUL E., "The Real Crux of Supervision," **Contemporary Education** 44:3, pp. 140-141, January 1973.

POLIVRA, JOHN B., "For Cooperating Teachers Only: How to Avoid the Communication Gap," **Social Studies Journal** 8:39-42, Spring, 1979, ERIC EJ 193 298.

Chapter Nine

SUPERVISING PARTICIPATION
IN THE TOTAL SCHOOL PROGRAM

It had been one of those long, dreary days when nothing had gone as planned. A fire alarm interrupted the timed examination, needed materials did not get duplicated as promised, Linda and Cristie had a big argument in class, and it had now started to rain outside. As dismissal time approached, a voice sounded on the intercom, "Teachers are reminded of the open house this evening. Faculty members should be in their rooms by 7:00 o'clock."

"The end of a perfect day," commented Miss Bennett, "Did they tell you about this in methods class?"

Brian forced a smile. The last thing he wanted to do was to return for the open house. He had papers to grade and then he had hoped to relax a bit. Turning toward the window, he inquired, "Do you think it would be all right if I did not attend tonight? I completely forgot about this and I planned to get together with some friends later this evening after I finished grading the tests. Since I attended the PTA meeting last month and met several parents, I wonder if I might be excused from this one."

Miss Bennett considered the dilemma and she could appreciate his feelings. He had been working hard and she knew the relaxation was well deserved after this trying day. She was also aware of the fact that the school administration was stressing loyalty to this program in order to encourage more parental participation by assuring them that the teachers would be present. Brian probably should meet some of these parents.

Miss Bennett took a quick check of the gray skies outside and softly inquired, "What did they tell you at State? Do they expect you to attend?"

"I don't remember that it was ever discussed," was Brian's instant response. . .

PARTICIPATION IN THE TOTAL SCHOOL PROGRAM: School Does Not End at 3:30

Teacher education programs made significant progress when they began to require a full-time student teaching experience which enabled the candidate to devote complete attention to living the life of a teacher. The block arrangement has allowed a student teacher to participate in the total program of activities both during and after the school day. The result has been a more comprehensive overview of the responsibilities of a teacher.

Participation gives the student teacher an opportunity for total involvement in school affairs. It is here that much of the formality of school vanishes and people reveal their true personalities. This hidden curriculum is that part of school life where students pursue their own interests and develop lasting skills and relationships. Student teachers must participate in the extracurricular program because this may be the most significant learning experience for many individuals.

Participation experiences permit a different type of interaction with teachers. As student teachers and teachers work together in activities, student teachers can gain a broader concept of a teacher's role. A student teacher can also make contributions simply by being available to work and by sharing some fresh insights. These kinds of associations should help a student teacher to develop greater awareness of what is involved in being a teacher. There may be a real learning vacuum if a student teacher does not have the opportunity to work with teachers in their extracurricular and professional activities.

Informal interaction with youth allows student teachers to see a side of the pupils that they are not otherwise able to see. One student teacher commented that she really got to know her students when she worked with them on the construction of a float for the homecoming parade. A teacher candidate who capitalizes on opportunities of this type can get to know students better. This enriching opportunity can facilitate adjustment to pupils in the formal learning situations and cause pupils to perceive that the student teacher has a genuine interest in them.

The participation experience is an opportunity for the student teacher to enrich the school environment. A student teacher with musical talent may be able to assist a student with practice; a physical education major may be able to contribute to coaching; and a student teacher who has had experience directing group activities may be of value to pupils who are presenting a program to a school assembly or community organization. The possibilities are virtually without limit.

Participation activities offer the best chance for the student teacher to see and be seen by the school and community. Administrators, particularly, may have little opportunity to observe the student teacher except through the contacts of professional and extracurricular activities. Other teachers and school personnel will have their best opportunities to know the student teacher in these situations. Most of the community members only see a student teacher at a school function. Attendance at faculty meetings and participation in school activities may give student teachers a glimpse of teaching that had never before occurred to them.

A student teacher may have a limited concept of the scope and contribution of the entire school program unless he participates in the total range of activities. Usually a student teacher will feel honored at being invited to take part in school activities outside the classroom. Such an invitation contributes to the development of team spirit. Participation will help the student teacher:

Get to know and understand pupils
Understand the types of learning that take place outside the classroom
Understand the demands that are made upon a teacher
Meet and interact with parents and other adults in the community
Work with other teachers
Learn about the purposes and functions of the school
Understand the role of professional organizations in teaching.

Case Study No. 57: THE STUDENT TEACHER IS RELUCTANT TO PARTICIPATE IN AFTER-SCHOOL ACTIVITIES

Ron commutes to your school each day from the campus, a distance of twenty-five miles one way. He appears to be enjoying teaching and his progress is satisfactory, but he has seen very little of school life after hours since he is actively involved in the social and political affairs of the university. When you suggest that he participate in some of these functions, he indicates a willingness to do so, but says the expense of the second trip and certain campus activities make it nearly impossible. What course of action do you take?

1. Accept his explanation and cease to ask him to participate.
2. Inform him that student teaching is not complete until he has experienced the informal portions of the school day.
3. Attempt to get him involved in some activity where he will be needed or rewarded.
4. Discuss the requirements for participation with the college supervisor.
5. _____

Comment:

Since the supervising teacher's responsibility is to prepare the candidate for the total teaching environment, he must be concerned with providing participation experiences. Ron apparently has not yet been able to see the opportunities that result from such participation and feels that he needs to attend to some details of college life. The general recommendation of most professionals would be to request that he become involved in the whole program of the school.

Questions:

1. What effects will there be upon a student teacher who is not involved in participation activities?
2. How can a teacher convince a student teacher that participation activities are necessary?

Case Study No. 58: THE STUDENT TEACHER'S AFTER-SCHOOL ACTIVITIES INTERFERE WITH HIS CLASSROOM PREPARATION

Todd has come to your school with an extensive background as an athlete. Because of a shortage of coaching personnel, he was asked to help coach the seventh grade basketball team. Todd was excited at the opportunity and welcomed the experience. The problem is that since he began coaching he has not seemed to be very well prepared for teaching. In the next conference you expressed your concern about this to Todd. He explained that he had been so thrilled at the chance to coach that he had been negligent in his classroom preparation. He also revealed that the actual reason for his entering the teaching profession is to use it as a stepping stone to secure a position as a college coach. What course of action do you take?

1. Ask Todd to cease his coaching activity until his teaching performance improves.
2. Tell him that most school corporations hire good teachers who can coach and offer suggestions to help him budget his time more effectively.
3. Explain that a teacher-coach's first responsibility is to his students in the classroom and

that he must establish his priorities accordingly.
4. Point out that this experience would probably have little effect upon his becoming a college coach.
5. _____

Comment:

Since the supervising teacher is responsible for preparing the student teacher for the total teaching environment, Todd's involvement in after-school activities should be encouraged. It will enhance his learning experience and help to prepare him for his future teaching assignment. However, it is also the supervising teacher's responsibility to insure the educational welfare of his students. If Todd's inadequate preparation is affecting the students, then it is the supervising teacher's duty to inform Todd and correct the problem.

Questions:

1. What is a good rule for establishing balance between teaching responsibilities and extracurricular responsibilities?
2. If coaching is the student teacher's goal, should a supervising teacher attempt to limit the coaching experience in any way?

PARTICIPATION ACTIVITIES: **Educational Smorgasbord**

The range of activities is usually extensive in any school where student teachers are assigned. Obviously a student teacher will not be able to see and do everything in the few weeks of supervised teaching, so priorities will need to be determined. Those activities that will be of most benefit in helping the student teacher learn about teaching should be of primary concern and responsibilities should be provided which are normally expected of a teacher. The student teacher should get to experience activities which are logical responsibilities for the future.

Although there is no one pattern of specific activities that is appropriate to all situations, the following list represents those experiences where student teachers can usually be involved:

Faculty duties
  Faculty meetings
  Hall and cafeteria supervision
  Homeroom responsibilities
  Reports and other required information
  Parent conferences
  Attendance at evening school functions
  Instructional assistance to individual students
  After-school rehearsals and practices
  Conferences and meetings
  Collecting fees and money
Professional activities
  Meetings of professional organizations
  Committee assignments
Extracurricular functions
  Athletic contests
  Student social activities
  Faculty social functions
  Drama activities
  Musical events

Participation in faculty affairs gives the student teacher the impression of being accepted and allows direct involvement in substantive activities. These kinds of experiences illustrate the demands made on teachers out of the classroom as well as demonstrate how teachers interact with staff and other persons associated with the school.

Professional activities are becoming more significant in teaching. Student teaching can provide a chance for a student teacher to actually see what the objectives of professional organizations are and how they achieve their goals. Such contact should increase understanding and allow the future teacher to make more intelligent choices in regard to his own future involvement.

The college background of a student teacher may help him to be a real contributor to extracurricular programs because special talents can be presented in more informal functions. School officials and pupils alike appreciate the fact that a student teacher volunteers to participate in extracurricular activities. They perceive that it is an index of interest and dedication to teaching, and pupils feel they get to know the student teacher better and that there is a personal interest in them.

Case Study No. 59: IT HAPPENED AT THE OPEN HOUSE

Your student teacher has worked hard with you in preparing for the open house for parents. There has been much discussion between the two of you about parent-teacher relationships. During the course of the evening you hear the student teacher discussing a pupil's progress with his parents in the presence of others. She was using such negative expressions as lazy, never does the right thing, below average, trouble maker, impertinent. The parents seem to be very concerned and make some loud rejoinders. Trouble may be coming. What course of action do you take?

1. Do nothing unless the parents seek your counsel.
2. Enter the conversation and make positive remarks to the parents about their child.
3. Apologize to the parents for the student teacher's actions.
4. Arrange a teacher-parent conference for a later time when issues can be explored.
5. _____

Comment:

It would seem that the immediate task for the supervising teacher is to change the situation from agitation to more professional dialogue. Otherwise, it will possibly be embarrassing for all parties. Option two seems to offer the best possibility for making a constructive modification.

Questions:
1. What kind of preparation should a teacher make in orienting a student teacher to parent conferences?
2. How can you explain the student teacher's frankness in describing a student's behavior to the parents?
3. What would you say to the student teacher during the next conference?

Case Study No. 60: THE STUDENT TEACHER CRITICIZES PROFESSIONAL ORGANIZATIONS

You and your student teacher have just left a meeting of your local teachers association which had not been too exciting. After a bit of idle conversation, your student teacher asks why you bother to participate in such a group. Don't teachers have enough to do without attending useless meetings of organizations which just extract money from the teachers and make a lot of noise about negotiations, contracts, and strikes? She wants to know what this organization ever did for young teachers. How do you react to her accusations?

1. Attempt to cite some of the accomplishments of a professional organization.
2. Ask her to get to know the organization better before making judgment.
3. Explain that the organization is not perfect but that it does make a positive contribution to education in general.
4. _____

Comment:

Professional organizations are becoming increasingly important in the lives of teachers. The student teacher's comment reflects a lack of knowledge of what an organization actually accomplishes. It would seem that she should have an opportunity to get to become more familiar with the goals and activities of a professional organization.

Questions:

1. What are some means for involving a student teacher in the activities of professional organizations?
2. What should a student teacher know about professional organizations?

Case Study No. 61: RESPONDING TO A STUDENT TEACHER'S IMMATURE BEHAVIOR

The school disco seemed to be a logical activity for Dennis to supervise since you had the responsibility for this function. It soon became apparent, however, that you had one more person to supervise instead of having an assistant. A few of the pupils gathered around him for a long time and he was enjoying the attention. The situation became serious when he began to dance with one of the girls. You are aware of the danger of too much fraternization but he obviously is not. How do you react to this situation?

1. Find some responsibility which will get him involved in a more responsible manner.
2. Call him aside and explain the possible consequences of becoming too closely involved with pupils.
3. Ignore the situation at present, but later explain the possible consequences of his behavior.
4. Attempt to redirect the disco into an activity where the student teacher will not be so vulnerable.
5. _____

Comment:

It would seem that the immediate task of the supervising teacher is to transform the student teacher's role from that of a participant to that of a supervisor. Otherwise, the situation may become more difficult to cope with. Option One seems to offer the possibility of having the student teacher change roles in a less conspicuous way.

Questions:

1. What might cause a student teacher to act more immaturely at a social function?
2. What type of briefing should be given a student teacher prior to his assuming a supervisory role in an informal setting such as this?

DIRECTING PARTICIPATION EXPERIENCES: **Interpreting the Menu**

The world beyond the classroom may not be as readily apparent to the student teacher as the classroom environment because little attention is normally given to it in professional preparation. Since most of the participation activities are non-credit for pupils and constitute additional demands on teachers, the student teacher may need to be made aware of the responsibilities in the extracurricular domain. There may also be little or no frame of reference in regard to the priorities which should be placed upon participation. The supervising teacher may need to explain the various activities and to suggest appropriate responsibilities. The following might serve as a checklist for consideration in guiding the student teacher's activities in participation:

Explanation of what is expected from the student teacher
    Discussion of student teacher interests
    Indication of teacher's own responsibilities
Normal expectations of teachers in participation activities
    Requirements as part of contractual obligation
Possibilities for extension of classroom work
    Clubs
    Programs
Scheduling events
    Who schedules
    Where they are scheduled
Guidelines or rules covering the various activities
Opportunities for learning through participation
Opportunities for contribution

The supervisor's responsibility could be described as that of informing and guiding. This involves the responsibility of seeing that the student teacher is made aware of the number of activities which consume a teacher's out-of-class time and then involves the student teacher in those situations which will be valuable.

Dr. Douglas was admitted to the principal's office prior to his supervisory visit to Brian's class. After a few preliminary remarks, he inquired about Brian's progress as a student teacher. The principal stated that he was doing quite well and that he was a good representative of the university. He observed that Brian was one of the few student teachers who attended the open house recently and that he is always looking for ways to make a contribution. He thought it was a good indication of interest that he stayed around after school instead of rushing to the parking lot to get away as soon as he could. He further commented that he felt that teaching skill is highly correlated with the ability to be successful in directing extracurricular activities.

Dr. Douglas indicated appreciation of the report as he scribbled a few notes for his records.

Remember:

The student teacher should be involved in the same kinds of activities as the supervising teacher.

Participation helps to give a student teacher the feeling of being accepted and needed.

Student teachers are exposed to a wider audience in participation activity than in a classroom activity.

Participation should be accompanied by reflection and discussion if the activity is to be more significant.

USEFUL REFERENCES

CHURCH, KENNETH R., "The Making of a Teacher: Guidelines for the Teacher Education Institution and the Cooperating Teacher." **Physical Educator** 33:26-9, March, 1976.

LIMA, JUDITH, "Two Views from the Classroom: A Student Teacher is Coming", **Business Education World** 53:20-21, Jan.-Feb. '73.

McATEER, JOHN F., "Student Teaching Supervision Roles and Routines." **The Clearing House** 50:161-65, December, 1976.

NEEDHAM, DOROTHY, "The Learning Connection: Teacher, Student Teacher, Child," **Teacher** 94:8-83, September, 1977.

SELBY, JEAN, "Me? Supervise a Student Teacher!" **Illinois Teacher of Home Economics,** 19: 76-8, Nov.-Dec., 1975.

Chapter Ten

LEGAL ASPECTS OF SUPERVISING STUDENT TEACHERS

On Monday morning Brian was at school early eagerly awaiting the arrival of Miss Bennett. When she arrived he excitedly shared with her a story he had heard during the weekend while back on his college campus. The reported story was that another college student who had completed his student teaching the previous semester had been named as a defendant in a court case. Co-defendants, in addition to the former student teacher, were his supervising teacher and the principal of the school to which he had been assigned. While Brian did not know all the facts of the case, the lawsuit was initiated by the parents of a child whose eyes had been damaged during a science class which the student teacher had been conducting. The parents on behalf of their child were seeking an award in judgment of one million dollars.

After relating this to Miss Bennett, Brian worriedly asked, "Can they do this? Can parents sue a student teacher and his supervising teacher?" Miss Bennett weakly replied, "I don't know," which was the most accurate answer she could give at the moment because she had given no thought to this matter. She added, however, "but why don't the two of us find out?" . . .

PROVISIONS FOR STUDENT TEACHING: What Does the Law Say?

The legal responsibilities that public school teachers must exercise in the supervision of their pupils have been rather well defined by the statutes of the various states and the courts. However, the legal status of student teachers and cooperating teachers in the supervision of student teachers assigned to them has been defined less clearly. There are several legal questions that may be posed in this area. Although the answers to some questions may be more obscure than desirable, a study of the state statutes, administrative rules, and judicial decisions offer direction in answering these questions.

All fifty states have some statutory provisions or implied authority for the establishment of teacher education institutions. Since student teaching is recognized as a fundamental part of teacher education and is an accepted practice in every school district in the United States, a logical assumption would be that each state would make legal provision for it. Research, however, does not support the above assumption. For example, in one study legal provisions for student teaching could only be documented for 36 states.[1] This study reported that twenty-five states have authorized it by statute, six by implication through other laws, four by administrative rule of state boards of education and one by an attorney general's opinion. Fourteen states appeared to be without statutory authorization to conduct programs of student teaching. Another study revealed similar findings.[2] This study showed that the individual states greatly vary in their legal treatment of student teaching.

Several states were found to have clear statutes, while other states had neither statutes, attorney generals' opinions, nor judicial decisions to follow. Two examples of those states that clearly have made legal provisions for student teaching are Illinois and Indiana. An Illinois statute under the enumerated duties of public school boards provides for:

"Agreements with teacher training institutions. To enter into agreements with those institutions to provide facilities for student teaching in schools of the district."[3]

An Indiana statute provides specific authority for student teaching assignments:

"Public school corporations are authorized to enter into agreements with institutions of higher education accredited by the training and licensing commission of Indiana, for the purpose of providing teaching experiences for students thereof preparing for the educational profession and for the services of persons working jointly for any such school corporation and any such institution."[4]

Even though several states have not provided for student teaching by statute, the authority of the student teacher to teach in the absence of such laws has not been a subject of much controversy in recent years. Many believe that any state which requires student teaching as a prerequisite for teacher certification legalizes student teaching in public schools by

[1]Fred Swalls, **The Law on Student Teaching in the United States** Danville, IL., Interstate Printers and Publishers, 1976.

[2]R. Craig Wood, **The Current Legal Status of Student Teaching in the United States,** Educational Resources Information Center, ERIC Document ED 127283, 1976.

[3]1961, March 18, Laws 1961, p. 31, Sec. 10-22.37, as amended.

[4]Acts 1969, Ch. 246, sections 1, 2, p. 972.

implication. This appears to be a valid argument. Nevertheless, a clear statute is still needed in those states that have not granted legal authority for student teaching. It is encouraging that so many states have enacted such legislation during the past few years.

SELECTION OF SUPERVISING TEACHERS: **Do Legal Requirements Exist?**

The requirements for the selection of supervising teachers vary. Only two states have statutes that speak directly to the question. Maryland[5] and Texas[6] have laws which require joint approval or selection of supervising teachers by the college or university and the public school district. Both states include the stipulation that an in-service improvement program for supervising teachers be adopted.

While not addressing the question of selecting supervising teachers directly, a statute in West Virginia authorizing agreement for the training of teachers speaks to the qualification of supervising teachers as follows:

"Such an agreement shall recognize student teaching as a joint responsibility of the teacher preparation institution and the cooperating public schools and shall include the minimum qualifications for the employment of public school teachers selected as supervising teachers."[7]

Rules of the State Board of Education of Florida require that supervising teachers be selected on the basis of training, experience, leadership qualities, and positions in the school.[8] The State of Indiana limits student teaching supervisors to those teachers who hold the Indiana Professional License (a minimum of three years' teaching experience and a master's degree) and requires that the final selection of the supervising teacher shall be the joint responsibility of the teacher education institution and the superintendent of the state commissioned school with the approval of the supervising teacher.[9]

[5]1975, Ch. 679.

[6]Acts 1971, p. 1488, Ch. 405, section 13.

[7]**West Virginia Code Annotated,** Article 5, Section 18-2-6.

[8]Rules of State Board of Education of Florida, Chap. 6A-5, 1980.

[9]**Teacher Education and Certification Handbook,** State of Indiana, p. 112, 1976.

The laws of several other states provide for agreements between teacher training institutions and public school districts. Qualifications for supervising teachers and the process of their selection are often parts of these agreements. Criteria of selection generally focus on degrees earned, teaching experience and special courses in supervising student teachers.

Case Study No. 62: WHO HAS THE RIGHT TO REJECT?

Your principal asks you to consider taking a student teacher for the second semester even though you had one during the first semester. You are reluctant to do so because you have not had much opportunity to work with several of your students. You further note that her background is marginal in the teaching area. After due consideration, you return the application to the principal and explain that you feel that the assignment of this student at this time would not be appropriate. The principal asks you to reconsider and explains that the girl's father has been a friend of the school and the university. He implies that some pressure will be brought to consummate the assignment with you. What do you do?

1. Reconsider the decision and accept the student teacher.
2. State your original position, explaining why you feel that the assignment would not be a good one.
3. Contact the legal department of the teachers' association for assistance.
4. Suggest an assignment with an unqualified teacher and offer to provide some supervision and to sign the necessary forms which verify that the assignment was completed.
5. _____

Comment:
The final authority for accepting a student teacher may rest in various places. The question may be a negotiated item in some states. Others may rely on statute or an attorney general's opinion. In most cases, the teacher has the last word. If a situation such as this occurs, the best procedure is to first check the legal aspects.

Questions:
1. Is there an ethical question as well as a legal question in this case?
2. Do pupils or their parents have any rights in this matter?
3. Based upon the content in this section, how many legal alternatives exist?

COMPENSATION FOR SUPERVISING TEACHERS: **What Are the Provisions?**

It is common for teacher education institutions to offer incentives to school districts and supervising teachers that cooperate in their student teaching programs. These incentives often are in the form of monetary compensation or tuition waivers. This practice appears to be specifically authorized in only seven states, five by statutes and two by attorney generals' opinions.

West Virginia's statute that permits agreements with public school districts in the training of teachers clearly provides that payments may be made directly to supervising teachers by stating in part:

> "The remuneration to be paid public school teachers by the state board, in addition to their contractual salaries, for supervising student teachers."[10]

Texas also authorizes payment of supervising teachers in a statute providing for the establishment of teaching centers which reads as follows:

> "There shall be paid to the public school district serving as a Student Teacher Center the sum of Two Hundred Dollars ($200) for each supervising teacher, to be an **additional** increment for such additional services to the annual salary of each such serving supervising teacher."[11]

While these two states authorize payments to supervising teachers, North Dakota law states that cooperative agreements for student teaching may provide that these payments may be made either to the school employees or the school District.[12] A

---

[10]**West Virginia Code Annotated,** Article 5, section 18-2-6.

[11]Acts 1971, p. 1488, Ch. 405, section 13.

[12]S.L., 1969, Ch. 180, sec. 1-3.

Colorado statute authorizes state colleges and universities to pay boards of education for the services of public school personnel in an amount not to exceed seventy-five dollars per full-time student teacher per academic quarter.[13]

In those states in which teacher education institutions make payments to cooperating school districts the question arises as to the authority of these districts to make payments from these monies to supervising teachers. The statutes of those states do not specifically address this issue and no existing case law can be found to give guidance. Attorney generals in two states have rendered conflicting opinions to this question. An Iowa attorney general gave an affirmative answer to the question[14] but the attorney general of Minnesota rendered an opinion stating that the supervising teachers could not be paid any portion of the funds received from a state university for this purpose because they would be receiving compensation in excess of that provided for in the district's salary schedule.[15] In some states the Social Security Administration has determined that stipends paid to supervising teachers are wages and are subject to social security assessment.

The State of Wyoming permits incentive payments in its statute which provides authority for school districts and teacher education institutions to enter into agreements for the purpose of providing field experiences in teacher education. This statute appears to be the only one in the fifty states that authorizes colleges and universities to grant tuition waivers for the supervision of student teachers in addition to authorizing a stipend.[16]

Since few states neither authorize incentive payments by statute nor state board of education administrative regulation, on what authority are these payments made? The primary answer seems to be that since teacher education institutions are empowered to finance their teacher training programs, they by implication have authority to pay these incentives. They will probably continue to regularly make such payments unless prohibited by specific statutes or judicial decisions.

---

[13]Cooperative Teacher Education Act; Amended; L. 1975, p. 729.

[14]OAG, June 5, 1936.

[15]OAG, No. 161604, Oct. 27, 1969.

[16]Laws 1975, Ch. 154, section 1.

DUTIES AND RESPONSIBILITIES OF STUDENT TEACHERS:
What Is Legal?

There is a great deal of diversity from state to state in regard to student teachers' legal responsibilities. The situation is further complicated by the fact that less than one half of the states have addressed the matter at all. Yet this is an important question to which supervising teachers need a simple, direct answer.

While not defining the responsibilities of student teachers two states, Colorado[17] and Wyoming[18] provide that they be cooperatively decided by representatives of the school districts and the teacher training institutions. An administrative rule in Kansas, while providing joint agreement, specifies that the supervising teacher shall be a party to this agreement and also gives more direction as to the student teacher responsibility by saying:

> "Building principals and cooperating teachers to whom the student teachers are assigned, in conference with the appropriate officials of the teacher education institution in conformity with the terms of the contract, . . . shall determine when and to what extent student teachers shall assume responsibility or enter into teaching positions in the assigned school. . . . Student teachers shall be under the supervision of the cooperating teachers and building principals to whom they are assigned, and shall not be expected to perform menial tasks or assume responsibilities not generally assigned to cooperating or other teachers."[19]

Two other states, Mississippi[20] and Nebraska,[21] provide for cooperative decision as to the student teacher's duties and, in addition, state that he may be granted responsibilities identical to those of regular teachers. While these two states expressly permit student teachers to be delegated the same authority as certificated teachers, other states require that they be granted

[17]Cooperative Teacher Education Act; Amended; L1975, p. 729.

[18]Laws 1975, Ch. 154, section 1.

[19]Kansas Administrative Regulations 91-19-11.

[20]Mississippi Laws, 1973, Ch. 343, section 1(a).

[21]Nebraska School Laws, 1975, section 79-1297 and 1299.

this authority. Oregon,[22] Maryland,[23] and North Dakota[24] specifically state this while Indiana[25] implies the same kind of authority in granting "other school personnel," which has been interpreted to mean student teachers, teacher rights including suspension from school and exclusion from educational functions. North Carolina[26] and West Virginia[27] provide that student teachers may exercise the same authority in the control of pupil conduct as regularly certified teachers. West Virginia goes further by allowing a student teacher under the direction and supervision of the supervising teacher to exercise the authority of a substitute teacher.

Other states have implied that student teachers have the same authority as certified teachers. The States of New York[28] and Illinois,[29] while not giving student teachers the same authority as certificated teachers, have provided that constant supervision of them is not required. An opinion of the attorney general of the State of Delaware states that while it is probably doubtful that a student teacher would be a 'competent instructor' in the same sense as a certified teacher, it is clear that a student teacher would be capable of properly supervising school premises. If a study hall monitor, or cafeteria worker, is sufficient to supervise pupils in their areas of the school facilities, then a student teacher with the additional training he possesses should be able to supervise a classroom of students.

> It should be noted, however, that we are speaking only of the situation where a student teacher is left for a period of time by the regular teacher assigned to that class. It would not be proper for the local district to place a student teacher in charge of a classroom indefinitely or for a long period of time, such as a week or more. This would be in conflict with the obligation of

[22]Oregon Revised Statutes, section 342.980.

[23]1975, Ch. 679.

[24]S.L., 1969, Ch. 180, sec. 1-3.

[25]Acts 1973, P. L. 218, Ch. 1 and 5.

[26]Department of Public Instruction, **Professional Laboratory Experiences in Teacher Education**, p. 19.

[27]**West Virginia Code,** Annotated, Article 5, 18A-5-1.

[28]As amended L. 1973, Ch. 538, section 1.

[29]1961, March 18, Law 161, p. 31, sec. 10-22.34, as amended.

the Board to provide properly for the education of the children."[30]

There are states which have been advised by their attorney generals that student teachers can perform only under the direction of a regular teacher. The Kentucky attorney general submits that a student teacher may not legally take charge of a classroom in the absence of the regular teacher because he cannot be employed by or receive compensation from the local board of education.[31] At a later date, another Kentucky attorney general stated that a regular teacher must be present in the classroom when a student teacher is teaching since the student teacher is not certified.[32] The attorney general of Iowa concurred in an opinion which stated that student teachers are given the opportunity to prepare and present lessons, but the supervising teacher at all times has a duty to exercise proper supervision over the pupils in his charge.[33]

The question concerning student teachers' legal duties and responsibilities is difficult to answer. The majority of the states offer no legal direction in the formulation of the answer to this question. The laws and legal opinions in the states that do approach this topic do not possess enough commonality to provide general guidelines. Many of these states either permit or expressly provide that the student teacher be granted a large degree of authority, while other states provide that this authority be very restricted.

Case Study No. 63: LET ME TRY MY OWN WINGS

Ted's student teaching assignment is approximately two-thirds completed. You have been pleased with his progress. His lesson plans have always been fully developed and submitted to you for approval well in advance. Except for one minor incident relating to pupil control, you have never felt compelled to interject yourself into his teaching activities. During Ted's teaching, while not becoming directly involved, you have remained in a position that enabled you to observe him and the class at all times.

[30]Attorney General's Opinion, Request No. S-296, October 19, 1972.

[31]OAG 63-269.

[32]OAG 75-70.

[33]1974-OAG6.

One day, in a candid comment, Ted said to you that he wished that for just one week you would let him "try his own wings" and teach as he wanted to teach without checking his plans and constantly monitoring what he was doing in class.

How do you reply to Ted?
1. Dismiss his suggestion as not worthy of being taken seriously.
2. Tell him you have been checking his lesson plans and closely observing his classes to keep him from getting into trouble.
3. Agree to his suggestion and apologize for not having thought of it yourself.
4. Clarify the reasons for your remaining constantly aware of his planning and presentation, including the legal risks which might result from your lack of such awareness.
5. _____

Comment:

Generally, the student teacher should be given some time to teach during his assignment when his every movement is not scrutinized by the supervising teacher. His self-concept will be enhanced if the supervising teacher demonstrates confidence and trust in him. However, it should be remembered that, ultimately, the supervising teacher is responsible for all that transpires in the classroom. Accordingly, it is incumbent upon her to at all times possess an awareness of the student teacher's activities with the class.

Questions:
1. Would this request be legal in the state where you teach?
2. Would the supervising teacher's responsibility be modified if a student teacher were permitted to teach as he wanted to teach?
3. Aside from legal considerations, are there any professional or ethical questions involved in this request?

TORT LIABILITY: **Who Defends the Student Teacher?**

Tort liability is grounded in the following:

Every person is responsible for his or her own negligent acts and, thus, teachers are responsible for their actions in relationships to their pupils.

Student teachers are quasi-licensed professionals and stand in a teacher-like relationship to their pupils.

Student teachers are responsible for their actions with pupils with whom they are assigned to work. The mere fact that they are not regularly certificated does not absolve them of this responsibility. A Kentucky attorney general addressing this matter in an opinion said:

"A student teacher may be held liable for his negligent acts or omissions the same as a regular teacher except that a student teacher's actions would have to be judged in the light of the fact that he is acting under the direction and supervision of a teacher."[34]

In Kansas a state board of education administrative regulation dealing with the legal liability and responsibility of student teachers states:

"Student teachers, while in the performance of their duties and responsibilities as student teachers, shall be legally liable for their own acts and conduct, and shall be afforded protection under the law, to the same extent as their cooperating teachers and other officers and employees of the school district."[35]

Some of the states have anticipated civil liability for student teachers and made provisions for it. Most of these states have provisions in their statutes on student teaching granting them the same protection as regularly certificated teachers. Iowa law states that students . . . shall be entitled to the same protection . . . as is afforded . . . to officers and employees of the school district.[36] Section 613A.8 of the Code of Iowa states that the governing body shall defend any of its officers and employees . . . against any tort claim . . . arising out of an alleged act or omission occurring in the performance of duty.[37] Thus, student

[34]OAG 75-70.

[35]Kansas Administrative Regulations 91-19-13.

[36]Chapter 260, Code of Iowa.

[37]Chapter 613A, Code of Iowa.

teachers in Iowa are agents of the school district and as such must be defended by the district against tort claims.

A New Jersey[38] law requires school districts in that state to defend student teachers in liability cases. Connecticut[39] and New York[40] have "save harmless" statutes which offer student teachers the same protection against liability claims as regular teachers. Illinois[41] has a statute which provides that school districts carry liability insurance to protect student teachers against liability litigation.

In addition to the previously mentioned states in which statutes mandate that student teachers be protected against liability charges, another group of states provide for coverage in other ways. Minnesota,[42] Maryland,[43] and North Dakota[44] have laws that authorize liability insurance to cover student teachers. Utah legislation requires that student teachers be issued certificates for the period of their assignments and provides that these holders are certified employees who shall be covered by the liability insurance program carried by the district in which they teach.[45] Statutes in Idaho[46] and Colorado[47] likewise provide student teachers with the same liability insurance coverage as that accorded to regular teachers.

A statute in Indiana provides for joint agreements between teacher training institutions and public school districts for the purpose of establishing student teacher field experiences. One section of this statute reads as follows:

> "SECTION 2. Each such agreement shall set out the responsibilities and rights of such public school corporations, such institutions, and such students or other persons."[48]

[38]L. 1965, c. 205, section 1; as amended.

[39]1971, P.A. 344, as amended.

[40]As amended L. 1973, Ch. 538.

[41]1961, March 18, Laws 1961, p. 31, sec. 10-22.37, as amended.

[42]Laws 1961, c. 225, section 1, as amended.

[43]1974, Ch. 703.

[44]S.L., 1969, Ch. 180.

[45]Utah Revised Statutes; 53-2-15.

[46]1963, Ch. 13, section 143, p. 27, as amended.

[47]Cooperative Teacher Education Act; amended; L. 1975, p. 729.

[48]Acts 1969, Ch. 246, Section 2, p. 972.

This quoted section could be interpreted to permit such agreements to contain provisions for the liability protection of student teachers. The model contract which has been developed to meet the intent of the statute reads in part:

"The School Corporation shall provide Student Teachers and Student Participants the same protection against liability arising in connection with their assignments and projects at the School Corporation as is provided for members of the School Corporation's faculty."[49]

The State of Ohio provides the teacher training institutions with the authority to secure liability insurance for student teachers in that state. The relevant statute reads as follows:

"The board of trustees of a state college, university, or state affiliated college or university may procure a policy or policies of insurance insuring its supervisors of student teachers and its student teachers against liability on account of damages or injury to persons or property, in respect to the acts of such supervisors of student teachers and student teachers occasioned by any incident occurring in the course of the performance of their duties during the period of their assignment to any school."[50]

It can be concluded from the previous discussion that student teacher risk from liability claims is real and that such risk appears to be no more or less than that of regular certificated teachers.

LEGAL RIGHTS OF STUDENT TEACHERS: **Do They Exist?**

The laws of the majority of the states are silent as to the rights of student teachers. However, approximately one-fifth of them have enacted statutes directly granting student teachers the same legal protection as regular teachers. Most of these states have used almost identical language in the applicable sections of their statutes. The Nebraska statute serves well as a representative one and reads as follows:

[49]Agreement Concerning Placement of Student Teachers and Participants by Indiana State University.

[50]**Baldwin's Ohio Statutes,** 3345.20.

"A student teacher or intern under the supervision of a certificated teacher, principal, or other administrator shall have the protection of the laws accorded the certificated teacher, principal, or other administrator and shall, while acting as such student teacher or intern, comply with all rules and regulations of the local board of education and observe all duties assigned certificated teachers."[51]

The key phrase in this and the other statutes, relevant to the discussion here is "protection of the law." While these statutes do not specifically explain the meaning of this phrase, student teachers enjoy the same degree of protection in covered areas as that granted to certificated teachers. The term "law" as used here would appear to include the Constitution of the United States, federal laws, state laws, and state board of education and local school district policies and regulations.

Another small number of states, while not granting the general "protection of the law" to student teachers, have provided them with the protection of workmen's compensation insurance to cover injuries arising out of and in the course of their assignment. Such protection has been given in these states by statutes and court decisions. Wyoming, one of the states granting it by legislature enactment has a law which is illustrative of those in other states and reads in part as follows:

"The student of teaching, during his field experience, is deemed an employee of the school district . . . for the purpose of workmen's compensation . . . insurance as provided for other district employees."[52]

Courts in two other states have granted student teachers the right of workmen's compensation. In a California case a student teacher was injured while supervising students on the playground. The Industrial Accident Commission held that the student teacher was an employee of the school district and as such was legally entitled to compensation from the school district in which he was student teaching if he were injured while so engaged. The supreme court of that state upheld this decision.[53]

In a more recent Michigan case a physical education student teacher, in the absence of the supervising teacher, was tossed

[51]Nebraska School Laws, 1975, Section 79-1298.

[52]Law 1975, Ch. 154, Section 1.

[53]**State Compensation Insurance v. Industrial Accident Commission of California,** 22 C.C.C. 212 (1957).

in the swimming pool by his students. During this time he was struck in one eye by his whistle causing loss of sight in the eye. The student teacher sued the school district in which he was assigned under the Workmen's Compensation Act. The Compensation Board granted him benefits and, upon appeal of this decision, the supreme court of that state upheld the Compensation Board.[54]

There are some interesting court cases concerning the rights of student teachers to secure assignments and their rights in dismissal from assignments. In a West Virginia case a student was denied the right to teach because of his reputation as a militant on and off-campus and the publicity he had received associating him with violent incidents at his teacher training center. This teacher training center had attempted to place him in several school districts, but they had refused to accept him as a student teacher. The student sued the West Virginia Board of Regents to recover damages for his having been deprived of the right to teach. A federal district court dismissed the suit in a landmark decision which reaffirmed school officials' rights to reject a student teaching candidate so long as customary procedures and uniform guidelines were followed in a reasonable and nondiscriminatory manner. Accordingly, a practice (sic) teacher is subject to summary rejection with or without cause, so long as it is not in retribution for an exercise by him or some constitutionally protected right.[55]

A federal district court, in a North Carolina case, also dismissed the suit of a student who had been denied application for a student teaching assignment by university officials who had serious questions about his character in terms of suitability for teaching. He had admitted to smoking marijuana and had been arrested for drug possession, a charge that had been dismissed. The court held that the university officials did not act in bad faith and were not arbitrary in their discretion. It further held that university officials are entitled to wide discretion in the regulations of the training of their students.[56]

In another North Carolina case, a federal district court held that the dismissal of a student teacher from his assignment without warning violated the First Amendment of the United

[54]**Betts v. Ann Arbor Public Schools,** 271 N.W. 2d 798, Michigan (1978).

[55]**James v. West Virginia Board of Regents,** 322 F. Supp., U.S. District Court, S.D., West Virginia (1971).

[56]**Lai v. Board of Trustees of East Carolina University,** 330F., Supp. 904, U.S. District Court, E.D., North Carolina (1971).

States Constitution, particularly freedom of speech, and due process of law under the Fourteenth Amendment. The student teacher had been dismissed because he made statements that approved the Darwinian theory of evolution, indicated his personal agnosticism, and questioned the literal interpretation of the Bible. The court in the decision set forth the following principles:[57]

a. North Carolina General Statutes Sec. 115-160.6 provides that, "A student teacher under the supervision of a certified teacher or principal shall have the protection of the law accorded the certified teacher."
b. The unpaid student teacher had the same right to protection as a certified teacher and should not have been relieved of his teaching duties for unconstitutional reasons.
c. The hearings afforded the discharged teacher with 20 minutes' notice and before a hostile ad hoc committee without eyewitness testimony, where factual inquiry was confined to brief questioning concerning a few unorthodox statements, denied due process and equal protection. (U.S.C.A. Constitution, Amendment 14.)
d. Although academic freedom is not one of the numerated rights of the First Amendment, the Supreme Court has on numerous occasions held that the right to teach, to inquire, to evaluate, and to study is fundamental to a democratic society.
e. The university and the Gaston school authority had duly agreed that he (the plaintiff) would have a term of practice teaching at the school in question. He had the reasonable expectations that this opportunity for practice teaching would continue until the end of the fall term as required by his university curriculum.

In a Missouri case the dean of a school of education administratively dropped a student teacher from his assignment after receiving criticisms from the student's supervising teacher and university supervisor. They reported that the student teacher's behavior and attitude were such as to prohibit his remaining in the assigned school. The federal court hearing this case held that a meeting which had been held in the office of the assistant principal prior to his dismissal was sufficient to meet due process requirements. In this meeting the student was advised that his behavior would be discussed and was

---

[57]**Moore v. Gaston County Board of Education,** 357 F. Supp. 1037 (1973).

given repeated opportunity to defend himself against statements made by his supervising teacher.[58]

In conclusion, student teachers in some states enjoy by statute the same legal rights as certificated teachers. In all states they enjoy the same civil and constitutional guarantees as all teachers and other citizens. Though courts are assiduous in guarding these rights, they are not absolute for they will always be balanced against the rational relationships of a given rule to school operation.

Case Study No. 64: JUST A SOCIAL OCCASION

Your student teacher's behavior was somewhat independent and she had presented some liberal ideas in her health class. This attitude led to an indiscretion which placed her future as a teacher in jeopardy.

The problem resulted within two weeks of the completion date of student teaching when the principal called you to the office and informed you that the superintendent had instructed him to dismiss the girl from school. It seems that she and Miss Smith, the gymnastics coach, consumed drugs with some students who were participating in a meet in another town. Although they were not the student teacher's pupils and the student teacher had not brought the drugs, the superintendent felt that this indiscretion should not go unpunished.

Since your student teacher's pupils were not involved and since her performance was satisfactory, what course of action do you choose?

1. Accept the decision.
2. Appeal for consideration of her performance.
3. Discuss the situation further with the student teacher and secure complete details.
4. _____

Comment:

This case presents the classic question of whether teachers are evaluated solely on their teaching skill or whether they are also held accountable for their moral influence on pupils. Obviously the student teacher created an error of

---

[58]**Aubuchon v. Olsen,** 467 F. Supp., U.S. District Court, E.D., Missouri (1979).

judgment and should be reminded of that fact. The question is whether she should remain and demonstrate that she realizes the impact of her influence or whether she should be isolated from further contacts with the pupils. The fact that she possessed a controlled substance cannot be ignored as well.

Questions:

1. Does a supervising teacher have any role in the decision?
2. Are there any civil rights violated if the superintendent's decision is carried out?
3. What can be said in defense of the student teacher?
4. What should a supervising teacher do if she is aware that her student teacher is consuming drugs?

SUBSTITUTE TEACHING: **Can a Student Teacher Legally Serve?**

This is a question that has gone largely unanswered by the various states. However, a few states do give some direction in this area. Kansas seems to be the only state which gives a definitive answer to this question. An administrative rule authorized by statute reads as follows:

"Persons may not act as student teachers in the schools of Kansas without valid student teaching certificates. Certificated student teachers are prohibited from serving as regular or substitute teachers in Kansas schools while performing student teaching."[59]

An attorney general in Kentucky was asked specifically whether student teachers could perform the services of a substitute teacher in the absence of the regular teacher. His rendered opinion was negative and is quoted as follows:

"Since the foregoing statute provides that a student teacher shall be subject to the direction and supervision of the teaching staff of the school district, we believe the legislative intent is that a regular teacher must be present in the classroom when a student teacher is teaching. We believe that a student teacher

[59]Kansas Administrative Regulations 91-19-4 and 91-19-10.

is not qualified or authorized to serve as a substitute teacher. A student teacher does not have a regular or an Emergency Certificate from the State Department of Education and is therefore not authorized to teach except under the supervision of a certificated teacher."[60]

A statute in West Virginia concerning student teaching appears to be very ambiguous and in the absence of legal interpretation does not seem to offer an answer to the question. A portion of that statute reads as follows:

"The student teacher, under the direction and supervision of the supervising teacher, shall exercise the authority of a substitute teacher."[61]

It appears that student teachers cannot be used as substitutes in Missouri and New York. Two regulations from the Missouri State Department of Education state that a student teacher is not to be paid a salary nor be used by a local district to reduce staff or fill a vacancy during the period covered by the student teaching certificate.[62] The New York statute indicates that the number of certified teachers shall not be diminished by reason of the presence of cadet (sic) teachers.[63]

In Delaware student teachers may serve as substitute teachers with the proviso that they be certified as such after having been recommended for this certification by the chief school officer of the district to which they are assigned.[64] An attorney general in that state has delivered an opinion that student teachers could be compensated for their service as substitute teachers.[65]

Case Study No. 65: SHOULD THE STUDENT TEACHER SUB?

Your principal meets you on Monday morning as you arrive at school and asks to speak with you. He reports to you that another teacher in the school called him at

[60]OAG 75-70.

[61]**West Virginia Code, Annotated,** Article 5, Section 18-2-6.

[62]Missouri State Department of Education, Form C-2, 1/6/69.

[63]As amended L. 1973, Ch. 538, section 1.

[64]Delaware State Board of Education Regulation, November 12, 1970.

[65]Request No. S-296, Oct. 19, 1972, AGO.

his home during the weekend to say that because of a family emergency he would be absent from work the entire following week. The principal tells you that normally he would have called some teacher on the substitute list but he remembered that you had a student teacher and he thought it better to use him. He says it will be a good experience for your student teacher and also it will be less trouble and expense than obtaining a substitute teacher.

What do you say or do at this point?
1. Explain to him why you feel the student teacher should not be used as a substitute.
2. Tell him you feel his is an excellent suggestion.
3. Offer to teach the other class yourself for the week, leaving the student teacher with your students.
4. _____

Comment:

Not only is using a student teacher as a substitute teacher unadvisable from a sound educational viewpoint, the legality of doing so is certainly questionable. Such practice is generally not authorized and school officials using it may be particularly susceptible to any liability claims which may arise.

Questions:
1. Does this request have any legal implications for a supervising teacher?
2. Does a teacher have an option of approving or rejecting the principal's request?

On Monday afternoon Miss Bennett and Brian met with Mr. Williams, the principal, to discuss the legal ramifications of student teaching that might relate to them. Mr. Williams, after apologizing for not dealing with this question at an earlier time with them, proceeded to describe the authority and responsibility of both Brian, as a student teacher, and Miss Bennett, as a supervising teacher. While walking down the hall following the meeting, Brian remarked that he did not think Mr. Williams had appeared very concerned when he had been told during their discussion about the million dollar lawsuit.

It is now Friday afternoon. The last students have left Miss Bennett's and Brian's classroom and they are unwinding from the day's classes.

Brian says, "Even though I am tired, I certainly feel more relaxed than I did when the week began. That story I heard about a student teacher being sued really had me upset."

Miss Bennett replied, "I must admit that I was somewhat apprehensive myself after hearing that story. However, following our talk with Mr. Williams I feel reassured."

Remember:

√Existing laws and regulations regarding supervised student teaching vary from state to state.

√The supervising teacher should be familiar with any applicable laws and regulations concerning student teaching in his state and school district.

The student teacher should be apprised of all legal guidelines which affect him.

There should be a clear agreement as to the precise duties and responsibilities of the student teacher. Parties to this understanding shall be the student teacher, supervising teacher, building principal or other designated administrator and college supervisor.

The student teacher is basically a learner and generally should operate under the observant eye of the supervising teacher.

√ The supervising teacher, not the student teacher, is charged with the care of pupils and their well being.

√ Any delegation of authority to the student teacher does not lessen the ultimate responsibility of the supervising teacher to the pupils.

√ It is incumbent upon the supervising teacher to be fully aware of the student teacher's planned activities and their appropriateness.

The student teacher, like any other teacher, is responsible for his negligent acts and may be held liable for them.

The student teacher enjoys the same civil and constitutional guarantees, (due process, freedom of speech, etc.) as do all teachers.

Using student teachers as substitute teachers is generally not legally authorized and is not recommended as a sound educational practice.

USEFUL REFERENCES

ASSOCIATION OF TEACHER EDUCATORS, **Providing Legal Status for Student Teachers,** The Association, 1900 Association Drive, Reston, VA.

DROWATSKY, JOHN N., "The Cooperating Teacher and Liability During Student Teacher Supervision," **Journal of Physical Education and Recreation** 51:79-80, February, 1980.

GRIFFIN, L. E., "Who Is Accountable for the Student Teacher: The Public Schools or the Universities?", **Journal of Physical Education and Recreation** 51:18, April, 1980.

HOFFMAN, CARL E., "Student Teaching Legal Status Varies Widely Among States, **Journal of Teacher Education** 30:7-9, July/August, 1979.

MACK, MICHAEL, **The Student Teacher and the Law,** Eric Resources Information Center, ERIC Document ED 102165, 1973.

MULHERN, JOHN D., "Student Teaching and the Betts Decision," **Viewpoints** 2:1, pp. 6-7, Fall/Winder, 1979-80.

SWALLS, FRED, **The Law on Student Teachers in the United States,** Interstate Printers and Publishers, 1976.

WOOD, CRAIG, **The Current Legal Status of Student Teaching in the United States** Eric Resources Information Center, ERIC Document ED 127283, 1976.

Chapter Eleven

PROBLEMS OF STUDENT TEACHERS

Miss Bennett and two colleagues attended a conference for cooperating teachers at State University. She welcomed this experience because it would be her first opportunity as a supervising teacher to communicate with teachers from other schools. The supervising teachers had been requested to spend one session sharing difficulties which they were experiencing in working with student teachers. She concluded that this particular session would be of little interest since she and Brian had encountered no serious problems. How wrong she was!

As soon as the chairperson opened the meeting for discussion, there was a barrage of complaints and requests for assistance. One teacher commented that her student teacher was lazy, and another complained that his student teacher was so busy with work and campus activities that he missed several days and was usually unprepared when he was in school. Miss Bennett shifted in her seat as she heard another teacher describe her student teacher's apathy, and she was really surprised to hear that two supervisors had been faced with the problem of student teachers who were absolutely incapable of working with pupils.

"You are all lucky," commented one teacher who had remained silent up to this point. "My student teacher proceeded to tell the class how easy it was to secure drugs." This was followed by a number of teachers who shared their problems on a variety of topics. The discussion time elapsed before all of the problems could be identified, not to mention being solved. Miss Bennett left the room wondering what she would do if she were faced with a problem student teacher. . .

STUDENT TEACHER PROBLEMS: **The Irritation of Growth**

Although student teaching is generally highly satisfying for all persons involved, this experience is not free from problems. These difficulties result largely from the rapid and intense change to which the student teacher is subjected. Student teachers should anticipate that some complications will probably arise and be able to deal with them in a constructive manner.

This chapter will address the major problems which seem to confront student teachers. Each problem identified will be described briefly and discussed in terms of how student teachers may be assisted in coping with such difficulties. No effort is made to structure them in terms of difficulty because the intensity of a problem usually depends upon the nature of the specific situation. A more complete and specific view of student teacher problems and their origin can be obtained by studying the chapter-end references.

Personal Problems

Economic Concerns

Student teaching is often more expensive than any other phase of a teacher preparation program. Charges for transportation and apartments may cause additional expenditure when a student teacher has to commute to or move to a community away from campus. Clothes and their care may be more expensive since teacher styles are not as casual as campus attire. Even the price of lunch may be a factor and incidental teacher expenses may be regarded as significant by student teachers. The results of economic problems may be shown through worry, fatigue, appearance, or avoidance of pecuniary situations.

Supervising teachers should make every effort to be understanding and should refrain from making requests which might cause financial complications for the student teacher. They may be in a position to offer money-saving ideas for their student teachers if the communication about the matter is open and frank.

Family Problems

Conflicts in this area may consume a wide range of possibilities. Some students may be adjusting to being away from home or from a spouse. In other cases adult-student conflict may be obvious when a student teacher and parents do not accept the same value system. Other instances may involve complications in marriage. Problems of this nature may affect the classroom behavior of a student teacher by lack of preparation, irritation or even depression. This syndrome may be extended beyond family and include relationships with members of the opposite sex or with peers.

This is an area where it is often difficult for the supervising teacher to render assistance. However, when it is apparent that these problems are affecting the student teacher's performance, they must be dealt with. It is important that the supervising teacher establish empathy with the student teacher and that they discuss the problem, if the student teacher is amenable to such a discussion. Generally, the supervising teacher should assume the role of a non-directive counselor in these discussions. In some instances the supervising teacher may not possess the counseling skills demanded by the problem situation and may wish to refer the student teacher to other school prsonnel with these skills.

Feelings of Inadequacy and Insecurity

This pattern of difficulties focuses on self concept and the ability to readily adjust to situations which may be potentially threatening. A student teacher who is required to teach in the presence of experienced professionals may feel inadequate. This may lead to frustration, withdrawal, apathy, nervousness, moodiness or depression.

These feelings can frequently be prevented through a planned set of activities which allows a student teacher to experience success and to gain respect. The use of positive reinforcement by the supervising teacher may help to establish desirable behaviors and to eradicate the more inappropriate ones.

Immaturity

The immature person fails to display the behavior that is appropriate to the role of student teacher. In most cases immaturity is apparent when the person resorts to the behavior which is acceptable to a younger group, most likely that of college associates, in order to gain acceptance. The person may possess all needed attributes for teaching except the ability to relate to pupils and teachers in an adult manner.

The symptoms of immaturity are not difficult to detect. One of the most exasperating types is the individual who dominates the conversation and poses answers to any complex problem that arises. Other behaviors include frequent, informal contact with students, appearance that identifies with the younger set, and a vocabulary that is frequently punctuated with popular phrases and cliches.

The immature student can change. A single activity or encounter can bring about the realization that change is needed. A frank talk may achieve significant results. There are several other procedures which can be successful in helping the student to abandon immature behavior. Consider the following:

*Help the student teacher be accepted as an adult by both
pupils and faculty.*
Encourage association with more secure teachers.
*Stay close to the student teacher in situations where immature
actions are likely to be most apparent.*
Expect and demand real contributions.
Monitor the student teacher's association with pupils.
*Require a student teacher to meet the same obligations and
expectations that teachers meet.*
Reinforce those behaviors which show symptoms of maturity.

Case Study No. 66: INSTANT EXPERT

Your student teacher likes to spend as much time as
possible with other teachers. The problem seems to be
that he is highly opinionated and seems to delight in
offering his views to faculty members. Due to this his
relationship with the regular staff members is strained.
Several teachers have come to you asking that you
keep the student teacher out of the lounge during
lunch. What do you do?

1. Ignore the situation.
2. Suggest that he stay away from the lounge.
3. Talk to him and explain that he must be more
   cautious about his attitude and conversation
   around other faculty members.
4. Suggest to the complaining faculty members that
   they tell him how they feel.
5. _____

Comment:
The request to isolate the student teacher is
obviously impossible. He must act more like a
teacher in order to be accepted. It appears,
however, that he is desperately attempting to be
accepted by appearing knowledgeable.

Questions:
1. What are some possible causes of the student teacher's behavior?
2. Are there other ways of helping him feel
   accepted without his having to pretend that
   he is an expert?

Case Study No. 67: THE STUDENT TEACHER MAKES IMMATURE COMMENTS TO THE CLASS

Your student teacher had been attempting to impress the class in a variety of ways and each attempt seemed to cause the pupils to lose more respect for him. A recent incident caused concern when he announced to the class that he was not prepared today because he was drunk the previous evening. He then began to tell what a great time he had. What do you do when this happens?

1. Take over the class because your experience should allow you to do better than an unprepared student teacher.
2. Let him continue hoping he will learn by the negative approach if his lesson fails.
3. Inform him of your displeasure and indicate that further comments of that type will not be tolerated.
4. Ask the pupils to write an anonymous evaluation of that class so far, assuming that they may convey ideas that will effect some change in his behavior.
5. _____

Comment:

The pupils will probably be tempted to make fun of his crude attempt to explain his situation, but it seems unfair that they should be subjected to ineffective teaching. There are some individual personality factors that will affect any decision, but it appears that an immediate non-threatening way of interjecting yourself into the class might be appropriate. This may force the student teacher to make some explanation after class and this may lead to productive dialogue.

Questions:

1. What would prompt a student to make an admission that he had been drunk?
2. What is the best way for a teacher to gain control of the class?

Problems with School Adjustment

Worry Over Possible Failure

Student teachers usually display the highest degree of anxiety in the initial days of student teaching. There are many contributing factors to this feeling, but one of the predominant causes is concern over success. Student teaching is often presented as the final test and a student teacher may initially feel unable to pass it. If so, the entire college program may be in jeopardy. A student teacher may either feel inadequate or have no valid frame of reference to evaluate performance. These feelings can create a lot of worry.

One of the best methods of coping with the problem is to make certain that some sort of success is experienced as soon as possible. If the student teacher quickly perceives that there is a chance of making it, many apprehensions should disappear making the student teacher more at ease.

Adjusting to the School

Student teachers may experience a kind of cultural shock when they enter school. They will be learning to adjust to a new way of life and to a new adult role. They may feel that they do not belong and this can result in confusion or conflict.

Supervising teachers need to be sensitive to the student teachers' feelings of not belonging or not accepting prevailing practices. One of the best preventive methods is to make certain that student teachers are aware of school policies and procedures. Sometimes it may be necessary to discuss their strong feelings and to help student teachers achieve understanding and a reconciliation of their divergent views. Student teachers should be included in as many aspects of the school program as is feasible so they understand the reasons for the existence of programs and policies.

Problems of Acceptable Appearance

The differences between the accepted patterns of professional dress in the public schools and the prevailing pattern on campus may create a breach that is difficult to reconcile. A student teacher may have some difficulty accepting the fact that appearance is a factor in teacher-student relationships. Problems usually center around casual dress and the difficulty which it may present in being accepted by faculty and students. It may not be easy for a student teacher to understand that it is sometimes necessary to dress more formally than teachers in order to gain the same degree of acceptance from students or to be distinguished between pupils and faculty.

There is great temptation to impose personal standards upon a student teacher without giving due consideration to individual preference. The criteria for judgment should be whether or not the student teacher's appearance affects professional relationships with pupils. If appearance must be discussed, the following guidelines may be helpful in approaching the problem.

The student teacher will usually prefer to have the supervising teacher discuss the subject.
An early explanation of school policy, if one exists, can avoid an inadvertent violation of the rules.
Reasons for standards or appearance should be explained.
Criticism of styles as such should be avoided if possible.

Physical appearance and dress in the classroom are somewhat analogous to the wearing of a uniform in that it is a symbol indicating that the person who wears it has certain skills, responsibilities, and authority. If a student teacher becomes aware that appearance can help to achieve acceptance as a professional person with a degree of proficiency and authority, the more informal patterns of appearance may be volitionally abandoned.

Case Study No. 68: THE STUDENT TEACHER CAN'T STAND RED TAPE

School policy requires that all purchases must be approved by the principal. Although your student teacher was briefed on this procedure, she has continually been critical of the delays in getting supplies for class projects. One day the principal comes to you with a bill for an unauthorized purchase. Your student teacher has purchased some supplies from a local store and charged them to the school. The principal says the school is not responsible for the bill. What course of action do you take?

1. Give the bill to the student teacher and inform her that it is her responsibility.
2. Pay the bill yourself.

3. Return the bill to the store with a note that a purchase order had not been issued for these supplies.
4. Ask the student teacher to return all unused supplies which she purchased.
5. _____

Comment:

The rules of the bureaucracy have proved to be too cumbersome for the impatient student teacher. She has managed to secure the desired supplies but the problem is that she has ignored the proper procedure for doing so. The orderly process seems confusing; thus, she has resorted to an unauthorized procedure which worked temporarily. The supervising teacher's task seems to be that of convincing her that it may be possible to secure needed supplies and yet work within the system.

Questions:

1. Whose actions are most defensible, those of the principal or the student teacher?
2. What viable alternatives exist for a situation of this kind?

Case Study No. 69: YOUR STUDENT TEACHER'S DRESS STYLE DRAWS ATTENTION

Your school has an unwritten dress code for teachers that calls for men to wear ties with a dress shirt and suit pants. Kenny, your student teacher, arrives one day dressed as if he is going to a discotheque. Although he does wear a loose-fitting tie with his satin shirt and tight pants, you feel that his appearance is not appropriate for the classroom. You notice, however, that several of the girls have complimented him on his outfit. How do you deal with this situation?

1. Ignore the situation as he will probably return to more conventional dress soon.
2. Inform your student teacher that he should not wear an outfit of that type again.
3. Discuss the situation with him in private and present the implications that may result from his wearing such attire.

4. _____

Comment:

The choice of clothes is a personal matter and dress codes for teachers have virtually disappeared. However, an individual, particularly a student teacher, should be aware that appearance can affect how persons respond to him. A student teacher should be aware that his appearance can either enhance or lower the perceptions that others have of him.

Questions:

1. Should a student teacher be expected to buy new clothes if he does not have clothes that conform to the informal dress code?
2. What guidelines should be used to determine acceptable appearance?

Problems with Adjusting to Students

Securing Student Acceptance

In most instances pupils have been at the school longer than a student teacher. Their patterns of activity are established and their relationship with the supervising teacher has been formed. A student teacher who enters the picture may not automatically be accepted by students. Attempts for acceptance may range from taking an authoritarian stand to informally associating with students. When problems of student acceptance are manifest, they usually result in rather complex situations. The classroom can become confused and disorganized.

A supervising teacher who suspects that student acceptance is a problem should quickly analyze the cause. Once this has been determined, a plan should be devised which will help the student teacher achieve recognition in positive ways. The negative student teacher should be made to see how this behavior may invite confrontation. The student teacher who attempts student acceptance by seeking to emulate their life styles should understand that leadership qualities are necessary for teachers. One very fruitful approach is to analyze the effect of verbal and nonverbal behaviors upon pupil behavior.

Opposite Sex Attraction

The narrow age span between secondary student teachers can lead to attraction between pupils and student teachers. A male student teacher may find that some of his female students are enamored with him. A female student teacher may be aware that some of the older boys are attracted to her.

Problems occur when a student teacher fails to react to such attention in a mature manner. A male student teacher may be flattered by the attention given to him by a high school girl and be tempted to find time to be with her. Such contacts may extend past the school day into evening and weekend meetings. In some cases the attention is a source of support in an environment where so much is demanded by the teaching and supervisory personnel. If the relationship becomes obvious, a student teacher will begin to lose the respect of students and may incur the displeasure of his supervising teacher or building administrator.

A female student teacher may find that male attraction is displayed through annoying behavior of some sort. It may appear to her to be a discipline problem and she will be likely to respond accordingly. She may find it hard to believe that such behavior stems from affection.

A supervising teacher will have to intervene whenever such problems start to surface. Several alternatives are available when consideration is being given to such a move:

Explain to the student teacher why certain pupils are reacting as they are.
See that the problem is discussed before it gets out of hand.
Alert the student teacher to sensitive situations.
Talk to the pupils involved and seek their cooperation.
Suggest how a student teacher can appear more mature in the perceptions of pupils.
Make your presence known in social situations.

Case Study No. 70: THE STUDENT TEACHER SEEKS THE COMPANIONSHIP OF PUPILS

The only serious problem which a new student teacher has is that of fraternization with his pupils. He enjoys being the center of attention and the pupils give him this opportunity readily. He spends many evening hours where small groups of students congregate. He is now gravitating to student company during the school day. You have recently noticed that his classes are becoming a bit too informal and feel that he may soon lose control because of this behavior. What course of action do you take?

1. Do nothing and assume that he will become aware of his behavior before too much harm is done.
2. Apprise him of his behavior and ask that he discontinue his informal conduct around students.
3. Attempt to structure his schedule more rigidly so that fewer opportunities for informal contacts exist.
4. Talk to the pupils and solicit their cooperation in helping him become more mature.
5. _____

Comment:

The student teacher may be receiving some personal satisfaction from the students that he is not gaining elsewhere. It appears that a more concerted effort will need to be made to draw him away from the students and into the company of teachers. Such a move should be made with as little fanfare as possible and should be accompanied by positive reinforcement. There appears to be a need for acceptance and it will have to be met by the faculty or the student teacher will likely continue to turn to pupils for it.

Questions:

1. What kind of responsibility could be given to get a student teacher more involved with faculty?
2. What is the difference between informal contact between a student teacher and his pupils which supports affective roles and that which may cause the learning environment to deteriorate?

Case Study No. 71: THE FEMALE STUDENT TEACHER IS ANNOYED BY A HIGH SCHOOL BOY

Lana likes most of the pupils she teaches but she complains that Bill is quite annoying to her. She says that he follows her around and keeps asking her questions or making comments. In class he seems to be either talking or creating a disturbance. She asks for your help. What do you do?

1. Explain that he probably is fond of her and suggest that she not become annoyed.

2. Talk with the pupil and ask him to alter his behavior.
3. Suggest she avoid him by appearing to be busy or by taking different routes so that he cannot intercept her so easily.
4. Tell her to be more firm in dealing with him.
5. Ask her to talk with the pupil and explain how difficult it is for her to teach with his acting as he does.
6. _____

Comment:

The first task is probably that of convincing the student teacher of Bill's actual motives. Once she is convinced of this fact, she might be able to devise her own method of dealing with the problem.

Questions:
1. What feelings are involved on the part of both parties?
2. What can be done to help the student teacher accurately interpret the situation?

Problems from an Overextended Schedule

Many of the problems affecting the student teacher have their roots in activities which consume time outside the school day. Such activities prevent the student teacher from devoting sufficient time to the teaching task. Unfortunately many of these outside diversions have deadlines and consequently their fulfillment seems more necessary than those demands of student teaching. The press of time devoted to outside responsibilities reflects in poorer teaching performance in several different ways. A student teacher highly involved in competing activities may display the following symptoms:

Inadequate preparation
Reluctance to go beyond the minimum requirements
Completion of requirements at the last minute
Absence from school
Fatigue
Boredom
Requests to be excused from meetings

Additional Course Work

The demands of an intensive college course can consume hours of time. The less explicit responsibilities of student teaching seem less important at the time than the immediate task of meeting course requirements. Students in classes compete for grades while student teaching offers either no letter grade or the implied promise of an A or a B.

A student teacher who is involved in a day-long program of teaching should be discouraged from enrolling in formal course work. In the event that such classes are necessary, it would be beneficial if the student teacher could relate some of the course requirements to the responsibilities of student teaching.

Part-time or Full-time Employment

The feeling of a financial necessity is very real to a great number of college students. Some may completely finance their education by employment; others seek jobs in order to live more affluently. The student teacher who has been able to work while successfully managing college responsibilities will likely anticipate that the same can be done in student teaching. He may not be prepared for the extra time demands required by this experience and may be convinced of the necessity for working in order to sustain his economic condition.

Part-time employment will almost certainly not enhance a student teacher's performance of professional activities. However, the immediate necessity of making payments can easily prevail over the more abstract rewards of a good student teaching experience. The conflict of demands for time can create serious problems for a student teacher.

College Activities as a Source of Problems

If a student teacher is assigned to a school close to the college campus, there may be the temptation to continue with normal social activities. Such participation competes for time but a student who is established in a social position at college may be reluctant to surrender some of that esteem to the uncertain promises of student teaching.

The supervising teacher should insist that the responsibilities connected with student teaching be given first priority. If campus activities claim too much of a student teacher's time, marginal or substandard performance is all that will be displayed during the professional experience.

Adjusting to the Problems of Outside Conflicts

A student teacher has too much at stake to deliberately risk a low evaluation of student teaching performance. It is not fair to permit a student teacher to jeopardize this report. When a supervising teacher feels that adequate performance is being thwarted by outside forces making demands on the student teacher's time and interest, it is suggested that the following points be discussed with the student teacher:

Learning about teaching cannot be accomplished by meeting the requirements at the minimum level.
A student teacher who is not thoroughly prepared is being unfair to the pupils.
The competing demands are only temporary while the results of student teaching are permanent.
The obligations of student teaching must be met.
A student teacher who indicates that teaching is secondary to other activities will be unable to gain the respect of pupils or faculty.

Case Study No. 72: THE STUDENT TEACHER WITH PROBLEMS RESULTING FROM EMPLOYMENT

Mark had worked several hours each week during his college years and this undoubtedly was part of the reason for his inadequate subject background. It took only a few days of student teaching to demonstrate the possibility that he might not be able to teach at the level expected for student teachers. In addition to his poor background, his grammar is inadequate, his organizational skills are weak, and he has virtually lost the respect of his pupils. You realize that he will have to spend many evening hours of work in order to succeed. When you inform him of this, he says that he does not have the time because he has an evening job. He wants to teach and he insists that he will do better as a teacher because he will not have to work part-time. What do you do?

1. Indicate that he cannot receive credit unless his performance shows marked improvement.

2. Adjust his teaching responsibilities downward so that he can continue working.
3. Require him to relinquish his job so that he can learn those skills which he will need for teaching.
4. Inform the college supervisor and leave the decision to him.
5. _____

Comment:

Apparently all Mark wants is a certificate so that he can teach when he is paid to do it. However, his overall profile would indicate that he is a marginal prospect. He may be using work as an excuse to avoid facing up to his problems in the hope that they will vanish or go unnoticed when he becomes a teacher. The main principle which must be considered in this case is whether marginal persons should be allowed to enter the profession.

Questions:

1. Are outside work and successful student teaching incompatible?
2. Are there guidelines which seem reasonable in considering whether a student teacher is allowed to work?

Instructional Problems

Instructional problems range from difficulties in processing cognitive matters through problems with technique. A number of difficulties relate to the inability to achieve sufficient student respect. The problems listed in this section are frequently the ones identified by student teachers and supervising teachers alike.

Difficulty Adapting to the Role of Teacher

These types of difficulties stem from some student teachers' misunderstanding of a teacher's role. They erroneously have an image of an ideal teacher and attempt to fulfill their perception of it. For example, their role concept may be that of an authoritarian personality who maintains rigorous standards. Problems result when they attempt to actualize these roles.

A supervising teacher needs to help his student teacher to be himself. Once a student teacher is convinced that each teacher has a unique personality, it becomes easier to concentrate on developing skills necessary to become a good teacher.

Planning for Instruction

The concept of planning is often quite difficult for a student teacher for several reasons. In the first place, several levels and several types of plans have been presented and it may be difficult to sort out the appropriate ones. Secondly, there may be some difficulty comprehending how the components of a plan, especially objectives, have any relevance for teaching. In the third place, they may have had little or no instruction in long-range planning, and the requirements for this type of organization may produce frustration. Fourthly, the ability to estimate the timing for an activity may be difficult in the initial days of student teaching. Finally, a student teacher may have problems understanding the necessity for planning when a supervisor teaches a class so well with no apparent written plans.

The supervising teacher needs to be sensitive to the above concerns and to encourage the student teacher to produce plans that will truly be beneficial in class presentations. Problems can often be prevented if the supervising teacher and the student teacher initially participate in joint planning and the student teacher gradually assumes greater responsibility. An effective rule for the supervising teacher to follow is to review the student teacher's plans far enough in advance to allow ample time for any necessary modifications before a lesson is taught.

Presentation skills

Student teaching is a time when teaching candidates develop skills of teaching. The skills which are successfully developed during this experience may be the techniques which will be continued into the early teaching years. Summaries of research indicate that three skills seem especially troublesome to student teachers: individualizing instruction, pacing materials properly, and finding a way to use variety in presentation.

Success in coping with these problems is closely related to planning and to the type of role modeling that is demonstrated by the supervising teacher. Students will probably need to be made aware of the theory of individualization as well as the various possibilities for individualizing the learning activities. In regard to pacing, experience will help, but review of plans can assist the student teacher in timing. Using variety in instructional techniques may depend highly upon the support and example of the supervising teacher.

Motivating Students

Student teachers want to be able to combat apathy, incomplete assignments, excessive absences, and other symptoms of the lack of motivation. They want to know how to secure the attention of pupils and to arouse interest in their studies. The problem seems to be that of process. The normal tendency is to use the traditional goal model,[1] i.e., if you do not conform, you will be denied grades, privileges, etc. Students may not respond to this type of motivation and see themselves motivated by the role model, i.e., "what can it do for me?" Student teachers must learn to take a more positive approach to student motivation.

Difficulties in motivation may be prevented or corrected through attention to the fact that teacher behavior influences pupil behavior. A student teacher must be aware of the potential for influencing students as well as have a knowledge of specific techniques which can be used for motivation.

Relating Subject Matter to Pupil Level

Student teachers often have an inadequate knowledge of their pupils' subject background and fail to understand that many of them are not as enthused as teachers about the subject matter. Thus, they often experience difficulty in adopting the subject matter to the needs and interests of their pupils.

In addressing this problem the supervising teacher should assist the student teacher in understanding that the subject matter must appear relevant to indifferent students and also be appropriate for all pupils.

Classroom Management and Discipline

This cluster reflects problems related to the inability of student teachers to maintain discipline. This is frequently identified as the most pressing problem of student teachers. This

[1]William Glasser, "The Role of the Teacher in Society," **Business Education Forum** 26:7, 37-42, April, 1972.

concern may reflect a number of feelings concerning pupil-teacher relationships. The same feelings about goal and role may exist as expressed in the paragraph on motivation.

Student teachers often need assistance in establishing and maintaining a structured learning environment. Concepts which have been learned in a college class may be hard to translate into practice in the presence of a noisy group of pupils. Supervising teachers may offer practical tips for coping but they will have to also assist teachers in understanding how discipline is actually established in the classroom.

Evaluation

The problems related to evaluation of instruction are numerous and include such matters as knowing whether a grade should reflect achievement or effort as well as trying to understand the value of giving grades at all. It is difficult to establish a comfortable frame of reference for evaluation. Initial test results are often disappointing causing frustration on the part of the student teacher.

A supervising teacher should monitor the evaluation process carefully in order to avoid an uncomfortable situation. In the final analysis, a supervising teacher is responsible for evaluation and must be able to defend the process.

Problems Resulting From a Lack of
Basic Teaching Skills

The normal term of student teaching will not be sufficient to warrant a recommendation for a teaching certificate for a small number of student teachers. Making decisions on incompetence is difficult, but the recent emphasis on performance criteria is making it simpler to identify and describe teaching behaviors. A lack in any one of the following traits could lead to a possible determination of inadequacy:

Personal deficiency such as timidity, insecurity, and immaturity
Lack of organization skills, including effective planning and failure to meet responsibilities
Lack of interest in teaching
Inability to work with people
Inability to communicate
Inability to manage a classroom independently
Inability to evaluate performance realistically

Inability to structure the environment in such a way that learning occurs
Seems to have little or no concept of the function of a school
Lacks essential teaching skills

Many of the above weaknesses can be improved through recognition and concentrated effort. If the problem is identified early and the student teacher is aware of it, a successful corrective plan may be devised. Although each problem needs an individual diagnosis and plan of action, the following procedures seem to have broad application in helping the incompetent student teacher to improve.

The supervising teacher works in closer proximity with the student teacher.
The student teacher and supervising teacher work together in classes.
The supervising teacher insists on thorough planning.
The supervising teacher inquires about other activities that might be competing for a student teacher's time.
The supervising teacher arranges for situations where a student teacher can experience some success.
The supervising teacher does demonstration teaching.
The supervising teacher provides continuous feedback including as much praise as possible.
The supervising teacher identifies problems early in the program whenever possible.

When it appears that little or no progress is being made, the college supervisor should be contacted. He can take the initiative in confronting the student teacher with the fact that performance is unsatisfactory. Sometimes his presence alone can be the catalyst which can bring about change. He may be able to motivate a student teacher or suggest a plan of action which will be of benefit.

The supervising teacher should document a student teacher's poor performance. If the difficulty is such that it can be identified on tape, secure a recording of the performance for the college supervisor's use. If a video-tape-recorder is available, it can be of value in documenting certain practices. Written information and other forms of record will give the college supervisor a better idea of what has transpired. The supervisor can work more effectively if there is a complete record of past activities and an accurate description of deficiencies.

The greatest oversights on the part of supervisors are

usually failure to keep complete records and reluctance to notify the college supervisor when incompetency is apparent. Closely behind these may be the failure to identify the problem early enough to permit any kind of remediation. Problems should be approached early in order to give as much time as possible for improvement.

Case Study No. 73: THE STUDENT TEACHER SEEMS UNABLE TO ORGANIZE AND COMMUNICATE

Eric was an indifferent student teacher who communicated poorly with pupils and faculty. His low grade index reflected a lack of command of subject matter. His oral presentations consisted of reading a few statements from the book. He never seemed to show any visible awareness that there was a group of students in the same room with him and he gave extended study periods where the students usually became bored long before the end of the period. He avoided conferences whenever possible and he never had any lesson plans to present. As Eric's supervising teacher, what do you do?

1. Discuss the weaknesses with him point by point.
2. Ask the college supervisor to recall him.
3. Team teach with him and delegate only responsibilities that he can execute.
4. Ignore the problems unless he comes to you for assistance.
5. _____

Comment:

The task of a supervising teacher is to teach a student about teaching. Eric certainly needs all the help that he can get. For the pupils' sake, it appears that the two may need to teach together with Eric doing what he can. As he improves, he can assume more responsibility. Sometimes the two may need to talk about teaching, and the supervising teacher may need to offer numerous ideas in order to get him started.

Questions:

1. Is it productive to work with a student whose skills are as poor as those of the person described?

2. Can you identify any methods which would enable the student teacher to see himself as he actually is?
3. Will a group of students be affected by a student teacher who is as poor as this one?

HELPING STUDENT TEACHERS WITH PROBLEMS: **Going the Extra Mile**

Each problem is unique and demands an individualized approach. However, it is important to note that it is helpful to approach each situation with a concept of how to study the problem and to be aware of a few specific procedures which will be helpful in working toward an acceptable solution.

Problem Analysis

One approach to a problem is to develop an analysis procedure which has some logic and consistency. Consider using the following steps for reference:

Step 1: Analyze the basic issues which affect the situation.
    a. What has happened?
    b. What principles are involved?
    c. Why did this occur?
Step 2: Consider the feelings of the people involved.
    a. What is the basic feeling of each person?
    b. Can you establish empathy (convince the participant that you understand the feeling regardless of whether or not you agree)?
Step 3: List and evaluate alternative courses of action.
    a. How will each alternative affect the participants involved?
    b. Are the alternatives feasible?
    c. Which will most likely prevent the situation from occurring again?
Step 4: Take a course of action that seems most defensible.
    a. Why is it a better alternative?
    b. How will it benefit the student teacher?
    c. Is it likely to prevent a problem from occurring in the future?

The style and behavior of a supervising teacher can contribute to the successful remediation of student teaching problems. Generally a positive understanding demeanor contributes to a better climate. The following behaviors are suggestive of such procedures and can be used as a point of departure in the development of a successful plan.

Discuss the problem with the student teacher in an objective manner
Treat the student teacher as a peer and not as an inferior
Demonstrate confidence in the student teacher
Provide opportunities for the student teacher to experience success
Encourage whenever possible
Be available for conversation and discussion
Be a good listener
Show a sincere interest in the problem
Know the facts before action is taken
See that the student teacher feels accepted and needed
Capitalize on special skills or interests
Specify plans of action which will possibly alleviate the difficulty
Try to put problems in proper context
Be flexible

The discussion of problems had been rather depressing to Miss Bennett initially, but then she began to realize that this background would probably be of benefit to her if she ever had such difficulties with a student teacher. She felt better prepared now in the event such a situation should ever happen in her class.

She returned to her school the next day wondering about Brian's solo experience. "How did it go yesterday?" she quickly asked.

"Great," replied Brian. "I was an instant success with them since I wore my western clothes complete with my cowboy hat. I told them how to secure grass without being caught, and I even taught them to sing a couple of songs that I learned at an all-night party."

Miss Bennett was temporarily confused until she spied Tom Larson, her associate from across the hall who had attended the group meeting with her. His innocent face immediately told the story. She broke into a smile, somewhat relieved to know that Tom had told Brian about the proceedings at the conference. She was inwardly convinced that a lot of problems could be solved if the supervising teacher and student teacher can be comfortable enough with each other to inject a little humor into the professional environment.

Remember:

The problem student should be given all possible opportunity to succeed.

Open communication is a great asset in the prevention of difficulties.

Many awkward situations result from incorrect and poorly considered reactions to a set of stimuli.

Problems often come to the forefront when success is denied.

It is better to prevent a problem than it is to solve one.

USEFUL REFERENCES

ALILUNAS, LEO, "Some Case Studies of Unsuccessful Student Teachers: Their Implications for Teacher Education Changes," **The Teacher Educator** 13:3, pp. 30-34, Winter, 1977-78.

BLANKENSHIP, JACOB W. and CUNNINGHAM, CLAUDE H., "Classification of Elementary School Student Teachers' Expressed Needs," **College Student Journal** 13:374-8, Winter, 1979.

CLOTHIER, GRANT, and KINGSLEY, ELIZABETH, **Enriching Student Teacher Relationships:** Supervising Teacher Edition, Midwest Educational Training and Research Organization, Shawnee Mission, KS, 1973, pp. 17-25.

COHEN, M. W., et. al., "Dimensions of Elementary School Student Teacher Concerns," **Journal of Experimental Education** 41:6-10, Winter, 1972.

GLASSER, WILLIAM, "The Role of the Teacher in Society," **Business Education Forum** 26:7, pp. 37-42, April, 1972.

HIGGINS, JAMES E., "The Trouble With Harry," **Contemporary Education** 47:241-3, Summer, 1976.

LOCK, COREY, "Problems of Secondary School Student Teachers," **The Teacher Educator** 13:1, pp. 30-40, Summer, 1977.

MORRIS, JOHN E., and MORRIS, GENEVA, "Stress In Student Teaching," **Action in Teacher Education** 2:4, 57-61, Fall, 1980.

MOTT, DENNIS L., "The Real World of the Student Teacher," **Business Education Forum** 30:5-6, February, 1976.

SOUTHALL, CAREY, and KING, DOROTHY F., "Critical Incidents in Student Teaching," **The Teacher Educator** 15:2, 34-36, Autumn, 1979.

Chapter Twelve

EVALUATING THE STUDENT TEACHER

Brian Sims' performance as a student teacher had exceeded Elaine Bennett's hopes. He was pleasant, cooperative, liked by the students, and well prepared in his teaching area. His plans were submitted on time and he seemed to be effective in teaching students at all ability levels. Since he was doing well, Miss Bennett felt that she might be doing a disservice to Brian if she delved into a great number of critiques.

She began to have some reservations about her decision after the last visit from Dr. Douglas, Brian's college supervisor. He inquired about the amount of time spent in evaluation, whether Brian was beginning to develop the ability to evaluate himself, and wanted to know if they had used the evaluation checklist in the university guide for student teaching. Her responses were brief and evasive because she felt that such procedures were unnecessary since Brian's progress was satisfactory.

Dr. Douglas stressed that the best evaluation occurred when there was frequent analysis of teaching, emphasizing strengths and discussing teaching problems. Although she did not protest to Dr. Douglas, she felt that such techniques might tend to cause Brian to lose confidence. Still she resolved that she would discuss this matter with some of the other teachers who had supervised student teachers, and she also intended to ask Brian about his feelings concerning the type of evaluation which he expected. . .

EVALUATION: Judgment Day, Pay Day, or Just Another Day?

The process of evaluating the student teacher is different from the usual evaluations that the supervising teacher is accustomed to making of his pupils. There are no quizzes, examinations, or term papers. An evaluation of the student teacher usually involves describing his competencies in many areas, using frames of reference in making these judgments that often are vague or limited. This is a difficult task for the supervising teacher but a critically important one. It is imperative if the student teacher is to make optimal growth during his assignment that he be given a continuous assessment of performance. Not only are regular evaluations important but the final evaluation often becomes the most coveted part of professional credentials.

The responsibility for evaluation rests primarily with the supervising teacher who devotes more time working with a student teacher than any other professional, understands the learning environment, and is in the best position to observe the performance of the teaching candidate. The student teacher generally places more reliance upon the supervising teacher's professional judgments than those of any other individual. If there is no assessment from the supervisor, a student teacher will be more likely to perform on a plateau.

Different approaches to evaluation are used in assessing student teacher performance and each reflects a different concept of the supervising teacher's role. Following is a description of three different approaches.

Subjective Evaluation - Judgment Day

A subjective approach involves a qualitative analysis of performance from the perspective of the more knowledgeable and experienced person who is sitting in judgment of the trainee. It is unilateral and leads more easily to dichotomous judgments with a student teacher often struggling to please the person who is judging. This type of evaluation points toward a terminal process, i.e., once judgment has been made, it is over. The final evaluation is the only evidence that attention was given to analysis of teaching.

Complete reliance upon a judgmental approach can create a good-bad syndrome where a student teacher may work for approval rather than for growth as a teacher. It places disproportionate emphasis on the final decision (grade, evaluation form, etc.) and may make both parties uncomfortable. Thus, a qualitative approach (Judgment Day) is not sufficient for a comprehensive program of evaluation.

Performance Assessment - Pay Day

The recent emphasis on teacher competency has made the quantitative approach more popular for the evaluation of student teachers. There are numerous lists of performance criteria which are available as standards for assessing teacher capability.

If a person possesses a given number of criteria, certification to teach is granted. This tends to provide specific evidence of achievement as opposed to the more abstract concepts implied in grades or written statements of evaluation. The stated criteria when accompanied by descriptions can help to focus on specific ways of achieving competency for teaching. This in turn can lead to analysis and skill development.

Although there are promising aspects of this approach, performance assessment can present problems. In the first place one must accept the premise that critical teaching behaviors can be identified and described by minute behavioral characteristics. The end result may be that an evaluation program is nothing more than a legalistic summary with some of the most important aspects of teacher performance omitted. It might simply become a process of verifying that some of the more simple teaching tasks have been completed.

Continuous Evaluation - Just Another Day

Evaluation should be just another day as far as the student teacher and supervising teacher are concerned. It should be an intrinsic part of the program in that it helps to interpret and to give perspective to all aspects of clinical activity. Evaluation should be as routine as teaching and should cover every part of the experience. In this vein, evaluation is a tool instead of an end product. It stresses analysis and reflection rather than criticism and faultfinding or reports of good and bad performances. A comprehensive program of evaluation involves an analysis of plans, procedures, alternatives, and implications so that teaching will be improved. Evaluation should not be considered as a final score; it is the game itself. To put it more formally, evaluation is a routine, essential part of growth.

The student teacher needs to be taught how to make valid judgments about his own teaching for throughout his professional career his improvement as a teacher will result largely from applying such self-assessment skills. The goal of the supervising teacher, therefore, should be to enable the student teacher to achieve an increasing ability to accurately evaluate his own teaching effectiveness. Hopefully, by the time he concludes his student teaching experience, he will have attained these skills of self-assessment. For this to happen, a considerable amount of time must be devoted to reflecting on and discussing teaching concepts.

Effective evaluation focuses on concern for a student teacher's progress in particular and the improvement of teaching in general. A simultaneous analysis of both is more likely to produce acceptance by the student teacher. If a student teacher approaches evaluation feeling that he and the supervising teacher are working on a problem, he should be more objective about the analysis.

In general, a continuous evaluation will illustrate the following principles:

The process should be designed to prepare the student to have a valid frame of reference for objective evaluation.
Evaluation should focus on those skills and techniques which are essential for good performance as a teacher.
Evaluation should identify specific areas that need improvement as well as recognize those that are of good quality.
Evaluation should provide guidelines for the next steps in learning about teaching.
Evaluation should furnish an objective description of the student teacher's ability and potential for teaching to a prospective employer.

A successful student teaching experience should prepare a teaching candidate to perform at a level that is consistent with minimum professional standards. The supervising teacher will be responsible for assisting in the achievement of that level of proficiency which will qualify the student teacher for entrance into the teaching profession.

Most teacher education institutions rely heavily upon the supervising teacher's judgment in determining whether to recommend the candidate for a teaching certificate. Within a relatively brief period of time levels of competence must be assessed in regard to the teaching performances listed below. The supervising teacher should be aware of them in assessing progress and in structuring the working environment of a student teacher.

The ability to manage a classroom independently as illustrated by performing the various tasks of teaching without dependence upon another person.
The ability to objectively appraise teaching in regard to human relations, academic background, and teaching skills.
The ability to structure the classroom environment so that pupils display evidence of knowledge and skill development.
The ability to understand the purpose of a school and the role of a teacher in that institution.
The ability to establish desirable and effective relationships with students, teachers, administrators, and parents.
The ability to identify, develop, and execute positively those characteristics which are recognized as teaching skills.

Case Study No. 74: THE STUDENT TEACHER FEELS THAT SHE IS RECEIVING TOO MUCH CRITICISM

You are aware of the various skills necessary for good teaching, and you are just as aware that student teaching offers a relatively brief period of time for the development of these traits. Unfortunately, your student teacher is going to need all the help she can get and you have been working to help her perform better. The full impact of your efforts is realized after a long conference where you identify a number of problems and she inquires, "Am I doing **anything** right?" What do you do?

1. Indicate that she is, but that you are attempting to help her improve in her areas of weakness.
2. Re-examine your concept of evaluation and spend some time discussing in detail those procedures that are successful.
3. Ask her what she thinks.
4. Indicate that when she shows evidence of self-evaluation, you will not have to provide as much input.
5. _____

Comment:

The tone of the case study seems to indicate that considerable emphasis is placed on the concept of Judgment Day, with little concern for making evaluation Just Another Day. It may be just as productive to analyze what was done well as it is to point out those areas that should be improved. At least it is desirable to discuss both aspects in order to present a more complete picture.

Questions:

1. What frame of reference should be established in approaching a student who has serious teaching problems?
2. What procedures can be used to help a student teacher to better understand problems?

THE EVALUATIVE PROCESS: **Making Evaluation Just Another Day**

Two requirements are necessary if the evaluative process is to be most effective. In the first place, the climate must be conducive to open communication between the supervising teacher and the student teacher. The following suggestions should prove to be helpful in meeting this requirement:

Offer suggestions for improvement or reinforcement of technique as soon after the experience as possible.
Focus on the activity instead of the person.
State suggestions for improvement positively.
Ask questions instead of listing good and weak points.
Use a variety of evaluative procedures and techniques.
Make the evaluation specific.

The second requirement is for the supervising teacher to possess a valid set of criteria which serve as a frame of reference for assessing teacher qualities. These criteria should be dominated by those skills and personal and professional qualities which are associated with teaching competency. Following is a set which can be used as a point of departure in the evaluative process.

Personal Qualities
 Appearance
 Health and vitality
 Poise
 Sense of humor
 Voice
 Interpersonal relationships
 Dependability
 Judgment
Professional Qualifications
 Commitment to teaching
 Positive attitude toward children
 Skill in use of basic English and computational skills
 Ability to reason and to solve problems
Teaching Skills
 Knows subject matter
 Handles routine procedures efficiently
 Knows how to evaluate pupil achievement
 Provides for individual differences
 Has classroom management skills
 Able to conduct class discussions

Case Study No. 75: THE SUPERVISING TEACHER FAILS TO RECOGNIZE SUCCESSFUL PERFORMANCE

You have a feeling of satisfaction with your student teacher's progress. She is meeting her responsibilities and making effective classroom presentations. Her relationships with the pupils are warm and positive, and she has shown initiative in planning related activities.

Since she is performing well you see nothing to criticize and feel that constant perusal may prove to be embarrassing to her. You become concerned though when you inadvertently overhear your student teacher complaining that she is upset because she is not receiving any evaluative comments from you. She indicates that you have said nothing about her teaching for two weeks. What do you decide to do?

1. Explain to your student teacher that you feel that her teaching is satisfactory.
2. Adopt a system where you concentrate on only one specific factor or quality at a time.
3. Review an evaluation form with the student teacher so that she will have a tangible appraisal of performance.
4. Indicate that you will concentrate on problems and will make such comments when you think they are necessary.
5. _____

Comment:

Silence may not communicate positive feelings to the student teacher in regard to evaluation. Although it is tempting to take acceptable performance for granted, it often needs to be reinforced. One logical alternative seems to be to initiate an inquiry with the student teacher concerning how she feels about her progress. This could then lead to your comments about her progress.

Questions:

1. What are some evaluative techniques that can be used on a continuous basis with student teachers who are performing at a highly competent level?
2. If a student teacher is progressing satisfactorily, what should be stressed in evaluation?

Case Study No. 76: REACTING TO A PARTICULARLY POOR LESSON

Your student teacher has just completed the poorest lesson that he has taught. He was impatient with pupils, talked too rapidly, and was incorrect in some of the facts presented. Since there are several problems, you will have to establish priorities and determine the best method of procedure. What do you do?

1. Record your various thoughts on paper and let him read your comments.
2. Plan an extensive conference session and utilize a set of key questions which are designed to elicit self-appraisal.
3. Concentrate on only one area at a time so that some improvement can be made quickly.
4. _____

Comment:

Obviously this situation demands some response from the supervising teacher. Before any move is made it might be beneficial to determine whether such performance is frequent. If this is just a one-day situation, it may not be as serious and may be due to such factors as lack of planning or loss of sleep. If poor lessons are recurring, a supervisor will need to take a more serious look at the problem. The approach may depend also on how the student teacher has responded previously to evaluative discussions and to how he perceives the supervising teacher. Several decisions will have to be made before an effective evaluation can be planned.

Questions:

1. Which of the problems should be approached first?
2. How can a supervising teacher establish confidence needed by the student teacher to make the evaluation effective?

Evaluation Highlights

The continuous evaluation procedure should be emphasized by at least two formal processes; the mid-term evaluation and the summary evaluation. Some teacher education institutions will require more frequent evaluations. The mid-term evaluation will likely focus on a set of criteria which are to be judged either formally or through an extended conference. The final evaluation will require the completion of a written assessment which will become a part of the student teacher's evaluation or permanent record.

Mid-term Evaluation

The midpoint affords a good opportunity for a more comprehensive look at the student teacher's progress. He has been in the school long enough for patterns to emerge but has enough time remaining so that concentrated effort can be devoted to improving teaching techniques. A comprehensive evaluation can be reassuring both in terms of progress that has been made and in allowing time for strengthening weak areas.

Some universities require a mid-term report. A discussion of this report can be enlightening for the student teacher especially if he is allowed to participate in the evaluation. Such a tangible form of evaluation can provide a great amount of reassurance for the student teacher as well as provide goals for the remaining weeks of the experience.

The Summary Evaluation

The summary evaluation will likely be in the form of a written report to the university. The discussion of this form between the supervising teacher and the student teacher may be the final opportunity for them to communicate formally. The student teacher will be vitally interested in knowing what the supervisor has to say.

A discussion of the final report can be a rewarding terminal experience for the student teacher provided that there are no last-minute surprises. The final report should be a summary of criteria which have been considered during the student teaching period. Such a conference should result in the student teacher formulating a profile which indicates both strong points and weaker traits. It can also serve as the time when recommendations may be made and discussed concerning the type of teaching position to pursue, the special skills which should continue to be sharpened, and traits which continue to need improvement.

The question concerning confidentiality of the final evaluation is often raised. Since 1974, when Congress passed the General Evaluation Provision Act and an amendment, commonly known as the Buckley Amendment, confidentiality of student teacher evaluations are prohibited in teacher education institutions receiving federal funds. The essence of the amendment is that students are given an absolute right to see education records maintained by the school.

Recent emphasis on the importance of student teaching evaluation has prompted concern about the right of a teacher to evaluate a student teacher. Case law seems to affirm the principle that professionals have the right, obligation, authority, and ability to evaluate teacher candidates. The only condition is that due process must be exercised, but this procedure may be vague to teachers. Worksheet Number Twelve in the appendix lists five processes which appear to constitute due process in student teacher evaluation.

EVALUATION TECHNIQUES: Choosing the Best Procedure

A supervising teacher who evaluates a student teacher must be articulate, specific, and understanding. Since evaluation can be emotional, an ill-chosen word or phrase can quickly create a negative mood and destroy rapport. The non-verbal cues may be more important than the verbal ones. In the evaluation process the goal is for the supervising teacher and student teacher together to assess performance with objectivity with the ultimate objective being that the student teacher's professional growth will be enhanced as a result.

Effective evaluation involves a variety of methods. The type of technique will vary with the task, the student teacher, the supervising teacher, available time and physical conditions. A student teacher who is open can probably be evaluated directly. The tense, insecure student teacher will require a more non-directive approach. Some ideas may need to be transmitted through written communication while others need to be developed through oral dialogue. There is no one appropriate procedure and a supervising teacher will have to choose the technique which seems to be the best one for the given situation.

Conference

The conference is one of the standard models for evaluation. This dialogue which was detailed in Chapter Eight will allow for brief discussion of areas of concern or for in-depth sessions which involve a considerable amount of time for discussion.

Written Comments

Written comments in the evaluative process seem to have a great amount of value for student teachers possibly because they seem to be more formal or permanent. They provide a tangible record of student growth and progress which can be periodically reviewed. Many universities will encourage some type of written communication between a supervising teacher and a student teacher.

Written comments can be made when conversation is not possible. This allows a supervising teacher to provide a more comprehensive reaction without having to rely on memory. Suggestions or observations can be more carefully worded for greater clarity. Such communication may provide a more beneficial way to offer criticism because written statements may be considered to be more objective than oral statements.

Written comments provide a record of continuous progress which can be periodically reviewed. This can provide an accurate record of growth and progress, or possibly the lack of it. For a thorough review of the use of written dialogue, see Chapter Seven.

Rating Scales and Analysis Forms

Supervising teachers may wish to use objective criteria which present a profile of student performance. There are many forms available for such use, although many teachers devise their own instruments. Judgments generally are perceived to be less arbitrary if they are reported on checklists or rating scales. One very positive argument for them is that they force the consideration of some skills and traits which might otherwise be overlooked. Another productive evaluative activity which can be developed through analysis forms and scales is the sharing of perceptions by the student teacher and the supervising teacher who complete the forms independently and then compare the results. An example of one university's rating scale is reproduced in the appendix as Worksheet Number Thirteen.

Audio and Video Feedback

Audio tapes can be used to present realistic feedback of the student teachers' verbal communication. These tapes can be particularly helpful in analyzing questioning techniques, word usage, voice inflection, and content organization. Cassette recorders are readily available in most schools and recordings can generally be made with a minimum amount of classroom interruption.

A video tape recorder is another helpful device to use in evaluating the student teacher. He can actually see as well as hear himself teach a lesson. A playback is sometimes all that is necessary for identifying positive teaching qualities or weaknesses. The picture can communicate reactions that frequently would otherwise not be apparent to a student teacher.

Pupil Evaluation

Pupil evaluations can provide a valid perspective on the effectiveness of a student teacher's performance in that they reveal the impressions of the persons who are being taught. Pupils may be able to make suggestions to the student teacher that the supervising teacher cannot convey successfully. Older pupils, obviously, can be more articulate in their evaluations than the younger children. To insure reliability pupil evaluations should be made anonymously.

The climate of the pupil evaluation is quite important. A pupil must feel that the student teacher is sincere and will attempt to incorporate valid suggestions into constructive action. Some student teachers have found that evaluation is more successful if it is projected, i.e., a student teacher asks for suggestions on how one of his particular classes should be taught differently next year so that the present students will not be affected by their statements. On the other hand, student teachers also benefit from mid-term appraisals which may point to changes which can be made immediately.

The student teacher's fear of pupil evaluations is one obstacle which will need to be overcome in using this procedure. The student teacher may suspect that the pupils will submit a number of harsh or unfair criticisms in an effort to get even. Other student teachers will be looking for praise only and can be quite concerned if there is even one poor evaluation. Once the student teacher understands the context of pupil evaluations there should be little difficulty in securing worthwhile appraisals.

There are many different ways of soliciting pupil evaluations. One of the simplest and most popular methods is the administration of pupil rating forms which can be completed quickly. These structured forms have the advantage of focusing on the particular concerns of the student teacher.

Perhaps the most informative and most revealing pupil evaluations come from open-ended questions such as the following:

What did you like best about the class?
What did you like least about the class?
If your student teacher were to teach this class again what changes should be made?

The open-ended type of question lets students express ideas in their own words. It is less restrictive and permits pupils to say that which is prevalent in their own thinking.

Self Evaluation

If a student teacher is to become a responsible teacher he must be able to evaluate himself accurately. He should begin to develop and refine this ability during student teaching. The procedures described above should all lead to the goal of self-evaluation.

A periodic independent self-evaluation can create worthwhile reflection on the part of the student teacher because consideration can be given to the formulation of the concept of what constitutes a good teacher. A student teacher can develop considerable insight through periodic review of events and feelings about his performance in the school. Self-evaluation at intervals of two to three weeks seems to provide good results. This span of time permits the student teacher to make adjustments following the previous self-evaluation and prior to the next self assessment. It also allows time for new experiences to have developed.

Case Study No. 77: EVALUATING THE STUDENT TEACHER WHO SEEMS TO DO EVERYTHING WELL

You feel that Laurie is doing so well teaching your classes that you find it difficult to think of her as a student teacher. There seem to be no areas where any type of criticism is warranted. How do you go about establishing any kind of evaluation procedures in this situation?

1. Concentrate on discussing why her teaching is so effective.
2. Examine your own knowledge of teaching to determine if you are correct in your assessment.
3. Attempt to create some problem situations which might extend the student teacher's ability to teach successfully.

4. Let Laurie's teaching experience proceed naturally.
5. _____

Comment:
Evaluation of teaching is seldom expressed in terms of what is happening to the pupils. Since the student teacher appears to be doing well, the supervising teacher should move into more sophisticated analyses of the results of Laurie's teaching. One such method is to consider what is happening to the pupils and why. This approach, focusing upon the product of teaching rather than the process, coupled with a rather sustained period of analysis may lead to a more meaningful assessment of the student teacher.

Questions:
1. What criteria should be used to determine that a student teacher is doing well?
2. What more sophisticated teaching techniques could be used by very successful student teachers?

Case Study No. 78: THE PUPIL EVALUATION CAUSES THE STUDENT TEACHER TO BE CONCERNED

Your student teacher decided to have his pupils evaluate the class using an open-ended technique. Most of the comments were constructive but three were very critical. The student teacher was quite upset by these. Although the negative comments were blunt, they did identify a problem or two which the student teacher could seek to correct. How do you discuss these negative comments with him?

1. Call attention to the fact that the vast majority of the class likes his work.
2. Attempt to help him to objectively evaluate the criticisms.
3. Tell him to ignore the comments as immature responses.
4. _____

Comment:
Perhaps a good beginning would be for the supervising teacher to let the student teacher

know that he understands his feelings. If he knows that the supervising teacher is aware of his thoughts, he may be in a better position to engage in objective appraisal of his skills. Ultimately, one would hope that the conversation would gravitate to a reasonable consideration of the specific complaints.

Questions:
1. What techniques can be successful in establishing empathy?
2. How can a few critical comments be put in context with the total number of evaluations?

Case Study No. 79: DECIDING HOW TO EVALUATE A STUDENT TEACHER WHO AVOIDS IT

You made a few early evaluative comments which appeared to disturb the student teacher. After this he seemed to avoid evaluation and you did not make a point of making further criticism. You realize that you soon will have to provide more evaluative assistance in spite of his objections or he will complete student teaching without a realistic concept of his abilities. How do you reestablish communication?

1. Discuss the matter with the student teacher and explain why continuous evaluation is necessary.
2. Return to the procedure of offering periodic evaluation without explanation.
3. Evaluate your student teacher but attempt to be more indirect.
4. Attempt to employ several different techniques in the hope that one or more will be successful.
5. _____

Comment:
The main principle to consider here seems to be that effective evaluation has to be continuous. The resistance may have resulted from sources ranging from the student teacher's feeling of inadequacy to a possible gesture from the supervisor which caused him to feel uncomfortable.

Questions:
1. What can cause a lack of communication to develop?
2. What techniques would probably be most acceptable to a student teacher in reestablishing communication?

Case Study No. 80: ESTABLISHING A FRAME OF REFERENCE FOR TEACHING

Before you realize it, the inevitable college evaluation form has to be completed. As you peruse this form, you see that some questions are going to have to be reconciled before you can make the appraisal. The source of confusion results when you read a checklist and discover that you have to check several criteria as outstanding, above average, average, or below average. Since you are not certain what degree of excellence is associated with these terms, how do you proceed?

1. Compare your student teacher with other student teachers you may have known.
2. Compare your student teacher with first year teachers of your acquaintance.
3. Formulate concepts for the terms and rate accordingly.
4. Forget about the possible definitions of the terms and produce a profile which identifies strong, average, and weak areas of performance.
5. Contact the college supervisor and seek his interpretation.
6. _____

Comment:
If a student teacher can leave his assignment feeling that he has a pattern of strengths and weaknesses just as all teachers do, then evaluation will have been successful. There is a feeling on the part of some students that any criteria marked less than perfect reflects poor performance. This is unfortunate, but it only seems fair to represent the student teacher as he is and not offer to the employer more than can be delivered.

Questions:
1. What is the typical profile presented on formal teaching rating forms?
2. Should a student teacher be consulted about his wishes in this matter?

Miss Bennett and Brian sat down to consider the evaluation report that she would send to the university for his record. It would be the last formal evaluative session, and both were relaxed and confident as they talked.

Miss Bennett began, "Brian I think you have excellent potential and I would be more than pleased to have you work here in Central City if there is a position available. You are poised and superior in establishing student rapport. You are certainly better than average in subject knowledge, use of voice, and creativity. Most of your weaknesses are in the areas of organization and in fostering more logical and creative thinking in the classroom discussions instead of seeking recall of facts. However, you showed improvement and will correct these difficulties as you gain experience. None are serious enough to cause any need for remedial action, of course."

Brian agreed, "I want to work on the techniques of questioning, and I must realize that these students are not as well informed as they sometimes appear. Organization has been a real problem for me, but I realize now how important it is for teaching. I agree with your analysis and would suggest that, if anything, you are too kind. I appreciate all the help you have given me in reaching this point in my professional development."

Remember:

The goal of evaluation is skill in self evaluation.

The conference is the core of the evaluative process.

Evaluation should involve a variety of techniques.

Identification of good and bad traits should be accompanied by an explanation.

Evaluation should begin when the student teacher starts teaching and continue throughout the entire time.

Evaluation is more than passing judgment; it is a process of honest interaction between two adults.

If a supervisor withholds his views concerning a student teacher's progress, the student teacher may interpret the silence as criticism.

The student teaching experience presents the final opportunity for teacher appraisal by a person who can observe performance over a sustained period of time.

Evaluation should stress growth.
Written student teacher evaluations should be prepared by the supervising teacher with the realization that the student teacher has access to them in the teacher training institution's records.

USEFUL REFERENCES

AICHELE, DOUGLAS B., and CASTLE, KATHRYN, **Student Teaching: A Cooperative Experience,** Oklahoma State University, 1979. ERIC ED 175 461.

BENNIE, WILLIAM A., **Supervising Clinical Experiences in the Classroom,** Harper and Row, New York, 1972, Chap. 6.

BOHNING, GERRY, "Subjective Judgment Pitfalls in Evaluating Student Teachers," **The Teacher Educator** 14:13-15, Summer, 1978.

BUETHE, CHRIS, and PETTIBONE, TIMOTHY, "Evaluating Student Teacher Behavior -- Three Views," **The Teacher Educator** 9:1, pp. 36-40, Autumn, 1973.

CHIARELOTT, LEIGH; DAVIDMAN, LEONARD; and MUSE, COREY, "Evaluating the Pre-Service Teacher Candidates," **Clearing House** 53:295-9, Feb., 1980.

CIAMPA, BARTHOLOMEW, **Working With Student Teachers,** 1974, Chapter 6. ERIC ED 194 892.

COOKE, BARRY F., "Pupils Can Help Teach the Teacher," **Curriculum Theory** 7:349-53, 194 892.

DARST, PAUL W., "Student Teacher Supervision with Audiovisual Equipment," **Journal of Physical Education and Recreation** 46:35-6, Sept., 1975.

DENTON, JOHN, and NORRIS, SHERRILL, **Learner Cognitive Attainment: A Basis for Establishing a Student Teacher's Competence,** 1979, ERIC ED 177 128.

FUNKHOUSER, CHARLES W., "Evaluating Student Teachers," **School and Community** 63:13, March, 1977.

GOLDENBURG, RONALD, and HAWN, HORACE, "Evaluation of Student Teachers: An Analysis of a Unique Approach," **The Professional Educator** 11:1, Spring, 1979.

HEROLD, WILLIAM R., "Evaluating Student Teachers by Means of Teaching Performance Tests," **French Review** 48: 1009-1012, May, 1975.

HEITZMAN, WILLIAM RAY, **The Classroom Teacher and the Student Teacher,** National Education Association, 1977, ERIC ED 146 152.

JAY, JUDY A., **Home Economics Education Handbook,** 1976. ERIC ED 135 934.

KENNEDY, EDWARD, "Gaining an Objective Picture of the Student Teacher," **Journal of Physical Education and Recreation** 46:44, March, 1975.

KNOP, CONSTANCE K., "Developing Student Teacher Skills in Lesson Planning and Self-Critiquing", **Foreign Language Annuals** 12:477-84, December, 1979.

KUEHL, RAYMOND, **A Taxonomy of Critical Tasks for Evaluating Student Teachers,** Association of Teacher Educators, 1979, ERIC ED 179 544.

LANG, DUAINE C., QUICK, ALAN F., and JOHNSON, JAMES A., **A Partnership in the Supervision of Student Teachers,** The Great Lakes Publishing Company, Mount Pleasant, MI, 1975, Chapter 9.

LANG, DUAINE C., and ALLISON, HOWARD, **Helping Clinical Students Self-Evaluate,** Professional Improvement Series, Northern Illinois University, DeKalb, IL, (slide tape).

McATEER, JOHN F., **Your Student Teacher's Final Evaluation** 8 pp. ERIC Microfiche No. ED 085 394.

MacNAUGHTON, ROBERT A., "Getting It Together," **Peabody Journal of Education** 55:82-9, Jan., 1978.

McATEER, JOHN F., "Student Teaching Supervisor: Roles and Routines," **The Clearing House** 50:165, Dec., 1976.

OTTAWA (ONTARIO) CANADIAN TEACHERS FEDERATION, **Proceedings of the 1977 Conference on Teacher Education,** March, 1977. ERIC ED 148 797.

SCOTT, GARY, **Writing Final Student Teaching Evaluations,** Professional Improvement Series, Northern Illinois University, DeKalb, IL. (slide tape).

TOM, ALAN, "The Case for Pass/Fail Student Teaching," **The Teacher Educator** 10:1, pp. 2-7, Autumn, 1974.

VOSS, RANDY, and ABRELL, RONALD L., "A Positive Appraisal Model for Competency-Based Student Teaching," **Clearing House** 50:31-8, Sept., 1976.

WHIDDON, SUE, **A Competency Chart for Evaluating Student Teachers in Physical Education,** 1978, ERIC ED 161 836.

EPILOGUE

The period of student teaching seemed to pass in an unbelievably brief amount of time. Brian Sims concluded his last day as a student teacher and said farewell to his pupils. He was unprepared for the emotional reactions of some of his students on this final day, and he was visibly touched by their expressions of regret that he was leaving. He conveyed his final appreciation to Miss Bennett and the other school personnel, vowing that he would keep in touch with them. He left Central School as a confident young professional who liked teaching. As he exited, he realized that he was a much different person than the insecure young man who timidly walked into the building a few weeks ago. At this moment he was convinced that this experience had exercised a more profound impact on him than any other block of academic and professional study at the university.

Elaine Bennett felt that she was a different person, too. She was certain that she was a better teacher for having had the experience of sharing her classroom with a student teacher. She had done a lot of reflecting about her own teaching during the past few weeks, and she had learned much from Brian. Her professional background also had been enriched due to the university contacts which had been initiated by this activity. Most of all, she felt that the presence of two teachers in the classroom caused her students to receive more attention. She may have helped shape the destiny of a young teacher, but she had also refined her own teaching technique. She allowed herself a final look down the hall as Brian disappeared into a crowd of students and then turned back into her classroom where she gazed for a moment at his empty desk. . .

BECOMING A SUPERVISOR: It Is Up To You

Brian Sims is the composite of many student teachers and Elaine Bennett represents hundreds of beginning supervisors. Both were as typical as they could be in illustrating what can be accomplished in an experience where no two situations can be alike. Brian's problems and achievements were the ordinary ones, and Miss Bennett made the moves which would usually be appropriate. Their example suggests that a teacher and student teacher who are aware of their roles and responsibilities can bring about decisive changes in teaching technique.

The content of the book was designed to broaden professional conceptions rather than to prescribe specific techniques of supervision. The number of possibilities for experiences are virtually unlimited. However, Worksheet Number Fourteen in the Appendix summarizes a number of typical activities of student teachers. The checklist can assist in assessing the totality of the experience and provide some direction for any future supervisory activities.

A teacher is a decision-maker who has to choose from alternatives rather than to rely on a pat response to situations which appear to be similar. Judgments are based on awareness of the dynamics of a given situation, the personalities of the people involved, and knowledge of practices and their effects. The inevitable outcome of his decision-making is manifest by the behavior of those whom he directs. The individuals who came under the influence of a teacher are now making our laws, manufacturing and selling goods to us, living happy lives, making and breaking homes, erecting buildings, consuming drugs, and guiding our children. The teacher is not the sole person responsible for molding our society, but there is at least one moment when this individual can touch another person in such a way that a life may be changed. One such opportunity for supervising teachers is presented in the student teaching experience.

The purpose of this book was to expand the teacher's concepts of options and techniques for guiding student teachers. The pages and chapters have been designed to increase the number of available options for making decisions concerning the development of a future teacher. Within a given context virtually any statement or procedure suggested in this book can be right, wrong, or irrelevant. The teacher must consider all significant factors and then decide upon an appropriate course of action. The more that is known about the field the better the possibility of making sound judgment.

The supervising teacher alone has to supervise student teachers. Other teachers can offer advice, and materials can provide background for making a judgment, but ultimately the decisions must be made by the supervising teacher. Success depends upon how well knowledge and values are applied in a professional situation. If they are put together correctly, a supervising teacher will have a significant impact upon teacher education.

APPENDIX

**WORKSHEETS
FOR
PROFESSIONAL SUPERVISION**

Worksheet Number One

CHECKLIST FOR A
STUDENT TEACHER'S ARRIVAL

The list below may serve as a guide for insuring that a supervising teacher has completed the activities necessary for a smooth beginning for a student teacher.

1. Prepare the pupils for a student teacher's arrival
   ____Inform pupils of impending arrival
   ____Tell pupils something about the student teacher
   ____Create a feeling of anticipation for a student teacher's arrival
   ____Other

2. Learn about the student teacher's background
   ____Subject knowledge
   ____Pre-student teaching field experiences
   ____Special interests or skills
   ____Other

3. Read the university student teaching handbook
   ____Understand basic responsibilities
   ____Comprehend requirements for public school supervisors
   ____Other

4. Become aware of legal status of student teachers
   ____Responsibility of supervising teacher when a student teacher covers class
   ____Rights and responsibilities of student teacher
   ____Other

5. Become familiar with school policy concerning student teacher responsibilities
   ____Reporting to school
   ____Absences
   ____Attendance at faculty meetings
   ____Supervisory responsibilities
   ____Other

6. Make a pre-teaching contact with the student teacher
   ____Letter of introduction
   ____Student introduction
   ____Acknowledge pre-teaching visit
   ____Other

7. Secure copies of materials to be used in orienting the student teacher
   _____School handbook
   _____Daily schedule
   _____Seating charts
   _____Other

8. Make necessary arrangements for student teacher to comfortably fit into the classroom
   _____Arrange for a desk or table
   _____Have necessary supplies for teaching
   _____Other

9. Secure copies of teaching resources for the student teacher
   _____Textbooks
   _____Curriculum guides
   _____Resource books
   _____Other

10. Develop a plan for the student teacher's entry into teaching
    _____Introduction to the class
    _____Introduction to faculty
    _____Initial teaching activities
    _____Other

Worksheet Number Two

PREPARING FOR THE FIRST FEW DAYS
OF STUDENT TEACHING

The following responsibilities usually must be assumed by a supervising teacher during the first few days of student teaching. This form may be used either as a planning guide or as a review of preparation activities in meeting these responsibilities.

1. Prepare for the special needs of the student teacher in adjusting to a different environment.
   Planned Procedures: _____
   _____

2. Introduce the student teacher to a class in such a way that status is given.
   Planned Procedures: _____
   _____

3. Place the student teacher into a partnership arrangement.
   Planned Procedures: _____
   _____

4. Introduce the student teacher to other faculty members and the administrative staff.
   Planned Procedures: _____
   _____

5. Acquaint the student teacher with the classroom routine and management techniques.
   Planned Procedures: _____
   _____

6. Apprise the student teacher of the class work which is currently under way.
   Planned Procedures: _____
   _____

7. Involve the student teacher in the activities of the classroom.
   Planned Procedures: _____
   _____

8. Provide the student teacher with a textbook and a place to work.
   Planned Procedures: _____
   _____

9. Orient the student teacher to the school building and its facilities.
   Planned Procedures: _____

   _____

10. Discuss school policies and regulations with the student teacher.
    Planned Procedures: _____

    _____

11. Assist the student teacher in learning pupil names.
    Planned Procedures: _____

    _____

12. Delegate responsibility and authority to the student teacher.
    Planned Procedures: _____

    _____

13. Plan for the student teacher's gradual assumption of teaching responsibilities.
    Planned Procedures: _____

    _____

14. Orient the student teacher to the community.
    Planned Procedures: _____

    _____

15. Help the student teacher to acquire background information on the students.
    Planned Procedures: _____

    _____

Worksheet Number Three

LIST OF BASIC REQUIREMENTS FOR
STUDENT TEACHERS

Many student teachers and supervising teachers feel that it is beneficial for a supervising teacher to list specifically the major requirements which will be expected of student teachers. For those who wish to develop such a list, the requests below can serve as a point of departure in determining a specific set of expectations.

1. Submit lesson plans in duplicate two days before they will be used.
2. Submit tests for approval at least two days in advance.
3. Prepare at least one set of grades.
4. Spend some time in the guidance office going over the files of the students.
5. Prepare at least one bulletin board display.
6. Utilize audio-visual equipment as follows:
   a. Review and show at least one film, operating the projector without assistance.
   b. Preview and show at least one filmstrip, operating the projector without assistance.
   c. Utilize the overhead projector in at least one of your classes.
7. Attend at least three extracurricular activities.
8. Write two self evaluations.
9. Have conferences with three students.
10. Observe 25 classes.

Worksheet Number Four

PERSONAL COMPETENCIES OF
SUPERVISING TEACHERS

Supervising teachers must be more than dispensers of knowledge. They serve as role models, facilitators, and counselors. The form below provides a set of self analysis criteria for determining the extent to which one serves as a supportive guide for a student teacher.

1. Accepts the student teacher as a professional colleague as evidenced by
   _____showing respect for the student teacher's decisions.
   _____allowing him to assume responsibility.
   _____permitting him to assume the same privileges as a supervising teacher.

2. Accepts the usual mistakes of the student teacher as evidenced by
   _____refraining from overreacting to mistakes.
   _____allowing the student teacher to continue with responsibilities.
   _____stating that mistakes are normal and not irrevocable.

3. Restrains from prescriptive directions as evidenced by
   _____discussing options with the student teacher before a decision is made.
   _____allowing freedom of choice on the part of the student teacher.

4. Conducts professional discussions with the student teacher, as evidenced by discussions about
   _____learning problems of students.
   _____teaching methodologies and their application.
   _____student behavior.

5. Allows a student teacher to observe and discuss the supervising teacher's activities and teacher effectiveness as evidenced by
   _____student teacher analysis of a supervising teacher's lesson.
   _____student teacher suggesting alternative procedures to the supervising teacher.
   _____student teacher records a supervising teacher's class on an analysis form.

6. Diagnoses learner's interests and needs, develops learning strategies and shares these procedures with the student teacher, as evidenced by

_____discussion of diagnostic procedures.

_____explaining why conclusions were reached.

_____explaining why certain teaching techniques will be employed as a result of the diagnosis and analysis.

Worksheet Number Five

ANALYSIS FORM FOR STUDENT TEACHERS WHO HAVE DIFFICULTY RELATING TO PUPILS

This worksheet may be used for a student teacher to analyze personal relationships with pupils. After the form is completed it may be used for review and for discussion with the supervising teacher.

                                                                    YES NO

1. Do I show sufficient enthusiasm so that my students are aware of the interest which I have in the subject?   ___ ___
Supporting information: _____

_____

Enthusiasm could be improved by: _____

_____

2. Do I insist that my students are courteous to one another and to me?   ___ ___
Supporting information: _____

_____

Respect could be improved by: _____

_____

3. Am I always courteous to my students?   ___ ___
Supporting information: _____

_____

I could appear more courteous by: _____

_____

4. Do I recognize good work as much as or more than I criticize poor student accomplishment?   ___ ___
Supporting information: _____

_____

I could better recognize good student work through: _____

_____

5. Do I make assignments that are clear and specific and justify those assignments in terms of their value to students?   ___ ___
Supporting information: _____

_____

I could make my assignments more acceptable to my students if: _____

_____

6. Do I make an effort to provide for individual
   differences?   ___ ___
   Supporting information: _____

   _____

   I could further individualize my teaching by:

   _____

7. Do I employ a variety of teaching procedures
   in order to avoid monotony and to appeal to
   student interests?   ___ ___
   Supporting information: _____

   _____

   I could improve variety and increase relevance by: _____

   _____

8. Do I attempt to make every student in my
   classes feel some personal responsibility for
   the effectiveness of my class?   ___ ___
   Supporting information: _____

   _____

   I could increase students' feelings of responsibility through: _____

   _____

9. Do my students really believe that my main
   purpose is to help them to learn?   ___ ___
   Supporting information: _____

   _____

   I could better convince my students that I
   want them to learn by: _____

   _____

10. Do I believe that my main purpose in teaching
    is to help students?   ___ ___
    Supporting information: _____

    _____

    I can further refine my beliefs through: ___

    _____

Worksheet Number Six

STUDENT TEACHER VISITATION REQUEST

TO: _____

FROM: _____

RE: Permission for Student Teacher to Visit Your Class

WHEN: Date _____

Period _____

or Hour _____

Class _____

_____ Student Teacher

_____ Supervising Teacher

If the above time is satisfactory, will you please sign and return one copy to the supervising teacher and keep the other copy for your records.

Sign here for approval _____

Worksheet Number Seven

GUIDE FOR WRITTEN OBSERVATIONS

An outline for Recording Participant Behavior and Lesson Structure.

I. The Teacher
  A. What image was projected by the teacher?
     1. Did dress, mannerisms, and general approach contribute positively to this image?
  B. Did the teacher move around the room, changing positions when the class changed pace or switched activities?
     1. Did these movements reinforce or distract from the progress of the lesson?
  C. Describe the teacher's speech in terms of volume, projection, inflection, grammar, and vocabulary.
     1. Were these characteristics appropriate to this class?
  D. Did the teacher's actions accurately reflect the announced purpose of the lesson?
     1. What were the most effective actions?
  E. Did the lesson give evidence of careful planning?
     1. Did it display a thoughtful and creative use of the resources available?
     2. Did it clearly fit into the current unit of study?
  F. How did the teacher conduct the class session?
     1. Was any time wasted by poor management?
  G. How were any discipline problems handled?
     1. Was there any apparent effort to avoid or eliminate disturbances?

II. The Pupils
  A. To what extent did the pupils participate in the class?
     1. What was the nature of their participation?
     2. Were students expected to initiate discussions as well as respond to questions?
  B. Were the students as individuals considered in the development and execution of the lesson?
     1. Did they participate in the planning and evaluation of the lesson?
  C. What needs and interests of the students were suggested by their behavior during the lesson?
  D. Did students work individually or in small groups?

E. Was there an appropriate balance between teacher-oriented and student-oriented activities?

III. Lesson Structure
   A. Did the lesson have a clear structure?
      1. Was its purpose announced at the beginning of the class?
      2. Did it follow a rationale?
      3. Was its purpose effectively carried out?
   B. Was the period divided into several activities?
      1. Were these activities well integrated?
      2. How did the teacher make the transitions?
   C. How did the class utilize homework or previous knowledge?
      1. Did the teacher make suggestions for further study and investigation?
      2. Was homework assigned as a natural outcome of the class?
   D. Was the time used to good advantage?
      1. Was incidental learning encouraged?
      2. Did the lesson plan have enough flexibility to capitalize on the special interests of students?
   E. Did the lesson relate to other courses, current events, or the personal interests of the students?
   F. Was the lesson successful as a whole?
      1. Why, or why not?
   G. How could the lesson have been improved?
      1. What alternatives could be considered?

Worksheet Number Eight

INSTRUCTIONAL OBSERVATION CHECKLIST

Teacher Observed .... Date .... Time: .... to ....

Observer .... Subject/Grade Level ....

I. **Physical Environment:**

    Conducive to learning (lighting, ventilation, temperature) Excellent ......|......|...... Poor

    Arrangements appropriate for activity? Yes..... No..... Alternatives possible? Yes..... No.....

II. **Lesson:**

    Objectives/intent explained to pupils? Yes..... No.....

    If yes, were they understood by pupils? All or Most ..... Some...... Few or None .....

    Motivational techniques used ....

    If used, were they? Effective ......| Ineffective

    Content taught ... .

    Related to other subject matter or previously learned material?: Yes..... No.....

    Procedures/methods (check as many as used) Lecture..... Discussion ..... Drill & Practice.....

    Independent study..... Small groups..... Laboratory   Discovery.....

    Learning center...... Role playing..... Programmed Instructional packages.....

    Question/answer. ... Other ....

    Activities related to pupils' needs/interests? Yes..... No.....

    Provision made for individual differences? Yes ..... No.....

    Appropriate for concepts/material to be learned? Yes..... No .....

    Variation of procedures/methods used: Excellent ......|......|...... Poor
    Flexibility or ability to adapt: Excellent ......|......|...... Poor
    Pupil participation: Active ......|......|...... Passive

    Presentation: Clear and understood ......|......|...... Unclear, pupils confused
                     Organized ......|......|...... Unorganized

    Use of reinforcement (check as many as apply) No reinforcement used..... Appropriate.....

    Inappropriate .... Positive..... Negative ..... Verbal..... Nonverbal..... Effective.....

    Ineffective .... Other ....

    Visual aids/instructional materials used ....

    If used, were they? Appropriate for activity(ies) Yes..... No.....

                  Meaningful to pupils Yes..... No.....

IV. **Management** of classroom: Excellent ......|......|...... Poor

V. **Evaluation:**

    Procedures used to evaluate pupil learning (check as many as used) Critique.....

    Pop quiz.... Formal test .... Question/answer..... Demonstration by pupils (on paper,

    at chalkboard, producing a product, showing skill, etc.)..... Other ....

    Were objectives/intent achieved? Yes..... No.....

    Will content/material need to be retaught? Yes..... No.....

    If yes, was there a plan to remediate? Yes .... No.....

    If yes, what was the plan? ....

Comments

Worksheet Number Nine

CHECKLIST FOR GUIDING PLANNING

The following procedures are recommended as ways of guiding planning more effectively.

1. Planning should be done cooperatively with both supervising teacher and student teacher suggesting activities and ways of working with pupils.
   Analysis of cooperative planning: _____
   Possible improvements: _____

2. The supervising teacher should acquaint the student teacher with his yearly plans, reviewing developments that occurred before the student teacher's arrival and projecting developments that will likely occur after he leaves.
   Analysis of planning review: _____
   Possible improvement: _____

3. The supervising teacher should explain his procedures for pupil-teacher planning.
   Analysis of pupil-teacher planning procedures: _____
   Possible improvement: _____

4. The supervising teacher should review the teaching plans made by the student teacher, raising questions and offering suggestions.
   Analysis of review process: _____
   Possible improvement: _____

5. The supervising teacher should provide evaluative sessions in which the student teacher gains skill in judging the effectiveness of his plan.
   Analysis of evaluative procedure: _____
   Possible improvement: _____

6. The supervising teacher should make certain that the student teacher's plans are submitted in advance so that they may be analyzed and improved if necessary.
   Analysis of advance planning requirement: _____
   Possible improvement: _____

7. The supervising teacher should encourage creativity and allow freedom in planning.
   Analysis of freedom to plan creatively: _____
   Possible improvements: _____

Worksheet Number Ten

COMPLETED TEACHER CLASSROOM ACTIVITY PROFILE

TEACHER CLASSROOM ACTIVITY PROFILE   STUDENT TEACHER _Kay Smith_ _____ Date _____

CLASS _Home Economics Junior High_ TYPE _____   SUPERVISOR _Scott_

Teacher Activity	Intel. Level	9:00 1	9:03 2	9:06 3	9:09 4	9:12 5	9:15 6	9:18 7	9:21 8	9:24 9	9:27 10	9:30 11	9:33 12	9:36 13	9:39 14	9:42 15	9:45 16	9:48 17	9:51 18	9:54 19	9:57 20	Approx. Min.	Approx. %
																						Summary	
MN Management - Non-Learning	1																					1	2
ML Management—Learning	1																					24	40
P Presentation	2																					20	33
R Recitation/Drill	2																					0	0
D Random Discussion	2																					5	8
LT Logical Thinking	3																					9	15
TP Thinking Process	4																					1	2

3 Minute Intervals

Explanatory Notes

1. Quiz
6. Distribute duplicated materials - Students read
8. Filmstrip "Good Diets". Teacher Interjects comments.
14. Question: "What do you think the purpose of the film was?"
14. Write down your meaning of nutrition
15. Students offer definition of nutrition
16. Instruction: "Write down what you ate yesterday."
17. Discussion of what was eaten yesterday
18. Question: "Do we really eat well?"
19. Pupils arrive at a definition of nutrients
20. Teacher presents a list of terms

Anecdotal Records

1. Do you think that an introduction to the filmstrip would have been of value?
2. Coordination of filmstrip and sound was excellent
3. Are there any ideas that should be summarized from the questions concerning the value of the film?
4. Are there any conclusions concerning the food consumed yesterday?
5. Good question - Pursue it further
6. The end of class did not seem to be a good time to introduce terms? Could it wait until the next class session?
7. Several different techniques were used. Students maintained interest.
8. Students were thinking. Continue to get them involved.
9. Circle arrangement of class seemed to create a good atmosphere for discussion.

Worksheet Number Eleven

EXAMPLE OF WRITTEN COMMUNICATION

| **Student Teacher** | **Supervising Teacher** |

IDEAS

How do you plan for discipline?

1. Always be prepared
2. Have at least three different activities each day.
3. Explain rules so that students know what is expected

AGREEMENTS

When do you want the bulletin board display ready?

Try to have it on the board Monday morning.

EVALUATION

I will work on that. The students gave little response to my questions, as you observed.

Questions such as, "How about roots?" are hard for students to answer. Try to be more specific.

Student Teacher	Supervising Teacher
What did you think of the introduction to the new unit?	You did this well. The students remained attentive. Word usage was at students level of understanding. The events were nicely coordinated. Did you notice that students needed more time to get pen and pencil ready? When there is time remaining as there was today, use it for review or for explaining the assignment.

PROFESSIONAL INFORMATION

Neal acted strangely today. Why?	He is being treated for a manic-depressive syndrome. He may not have taken his medication today.

Student Teacher   **Supervising Teacher**

THINKING ABOUT TEACHING

John is not making any progress. I wonder if persons like him should even attend school.

In spite of poor academic work, he is acquiring attitudes and values. This is part of teaching, too.

DETAILS AND PROCEDURES

Thank you.

1. Get the attendance check out by 8:15.
2. See that the door is closed (noise down the hall).
3. Let pupils at the end of each row pass the books. This saves time.
4. Check window shades on sunny days.

Worksheet Number Twelve

**DUE PROCESS IN
STUDENT TEACHER EVALUATION**

1. Review the evaluative instrument and its interpretation with the student teacher.
    a. Explain to the student teacher what each of the factors on the evaluation form means.
    b. Indicate what is expected from the student teacher.
2. Observe the student teacher.
    a. Indicate in the report the approximate amount of time or number of observations made.
3. Critique and analyze the student teacher.
    a. Inform the student teacher of any inadequacies so that he may take remedial action.
4. Evaluate the student teacher continuously.
5. Discuss the completed final evaluation form with the student teacher.

Worksheet Number Thirteen

SAMPLE STUDENT TEACHER EVALUATION FORM

Student Teacher _____   Subject _____   Date _____

School _____   School District _____   City _____

I. School Environment and Supervisor Contact : (Place an X before each appropriate word.)

A. Type of community: ___ inner city, ___ city, ___ suburban, ___ small town, ___ rural, ___ other ___

B. Grade levels taught: ___ elem., ___ mid. school, ___ jr. high, ___ sr. high.   C. Description of classes taught: ___ low, ___ high, ___ mixed.

D. Organization: ___ departmentalized, ___ team, ___ open concept, ___ other ___

E. Other significant activities in which the student teacher participated: _____

II. Evaluation profile based on observation of student teacher. (Check each item in one column only.)

Academic and Instructional Competence	Outstanding	Above Average	Average	Below Average	Poor	No Basis For Judgment
Teaching Skill:						
Presenting content						
Questioning techniques						
Evaluating achievement						
Motivating students						
Directing learning activities						
Professional Competence:						
Knowledge and understanding of subject matter						
Planning and organization						
Classroom discipline						
Record keeping						
Recognition of individual differences						
Demonstration of ethical behavior						
Selection and use of instructional media						

Personal Characteristics and Interpersonal Relationships	Outstanding	Above Average	Average	Below Average	Poor	No Basis For Judgment
Appearance						
Voice qualities						
English usage—oral/written						
Maturity						
Self-confidence and poise						
Enthusiasm						
Responsibility						
Flexibility						
Relationship with students						
Relationship with faculty						
Relationship with supervising teacher						
Reaction to suggestions and criticism						
Self evaluation						
SUMMARY EVALUATION						

III. Comments. Include evaluative, elaborative, and supportive comments concerning the student teacher's strengths, areas needing improvement, and growth pattern during student teaching.

Worksheet Number Fourteen

FINAL CHECKLIST OF
STUDENT TEACHER ACTIVITIES

How complete was the student teaching experience? Listed below are a number of activities which are considered to be beneficial for student teachers. Although every experience cannot provide activities in all areas, the checklist below can serve as a guide in assessing the extent of a student teacher's involvement and in projecting activities for future student teachers.

	Adequate	Less than Adequate	Notes
Planning and Organization			
1. Prepared unit plans.			
2. Prepared daily plans for a minimum of four consecutive weeks.			
3. Located and used supplemental reference materials			
4. Prepared a file of resource materials			
5. Studied student records			
Teaching and Analysis			
6. Practiced at least five techniques of teaching whole groups			
7. Worked with individuals and small groups			
8. Used a variety of media devices			
9. Video and audio taped one or more lessons and studied the playback			
10. Taught several classes without the supervising teacher being present			
Classroom Management and Discipline			
11. Prepared a seating chart			
12. Learned pupil names quickly			
13. Shared in routine teaching skills, i.e., roll, attendance			
14. Regulated temperature, lighting, and other physical aspects of the room			
15. Helped with disciplinary problems			
Conferences			
16. Conferred regularly with supervising teacher			

	Adequate	Less than Adequate	Notes
17. Conferences covered a wide range of topics related to teaching			
18. Conferred with the university supervisor			
19. Conferred with parents			
20. Used conferences as one method of evaluating teaching process			
Observations			
21. Observed a number of teachers			
22. Observed during the entire block of time			
23. Observed in more than one school			
24. Observed different subject and age levels			
25. Showed evidence of teaching improvement through observation			
Participation			
26. Attended activities and functions in the community			
27. Assisted with extraclass activities			
28. Helped supervise playground, cafeteria, and corridors			
29. Participated in pupil groups such as home rooms and clubs			
30. Contributed unique skills to the extraclass settings			
Faculty and Administrative Participation			
31. Learned about the work of special teachers			
32. Learned about the responsibilities of other staff members			
33. Attended faculty meetings			
34. Became acquainted with a cross section of the faculty			
35. Conferred with the building administrator			
Professional Activities			
36. Discussed pupil records with guidance personnel			
37. Participated in professional meetings			
38. Studied a teacher code of ethics			
39. Became familiar with professional journals			
40. Learned about the role of teacher associations and unions			
Evaluation			
41. Prepared, administered, and scored classroom tests			

	Adequate	Less than Adequate	Notes
42. Evaluated homework and other assignments			
43. Kept a grade book and built a record of work completed by pupils			
44. Assisted in determining and reporting pupil progress			
45. Learned to evaluate self			
Miscellaneous			
46. Became aware of the legal aspects of student teaching and student teaching supervision			
47. Became aware of the legal aspects of teaching			
48. Made a case study of one or more pupils			
49. Examined several textbooks			
50. Displayed adequate skills in using chalkboard			

INDEX

244